PREFACE

THIS book was born from a desire to capture the quirks, idiosyncrasies and piquancies of Malaysian life. Malaysia is a land of many races, each with its own language, culture and way of life. We should respect our differences, cherish our diversity and celebrate the commonalities that bind us. And as our cultures interact and embrace, a distinctive, uniquely Malaysian culture is evolving. It is a warm, wonderful culture, which only fellow Malaysians and foreigners who have lived here long enough can recognise. Nothing much has been recorded of it. This book therefore attempts to do so in its own special way.

Some Malaysian traits are positively endearing, some quite amusing (especially the way English is spoken here), and some really 'one kind' (such as the driving habits of Malaysians). I wanted to record some of these in a way that would entertain and, at the same time, make Malaysians aware and be proud of their cultural make-up, and to be able to laugh at themselves. Interlaced amongst the stories on Malaysian traits and lifestyles are stories from my personal experiences.

This book is not an academic discussion of the concept of Malaysian-ness. Nor is it comprehensive in any way in touching on the theme of being Malaysian as I write only from my angle, my experiences. It is a compilation of stories written out of love for my fellow Malaysians and pride in my Malaysian identity.

If this book can bring a smile or a sigh to your lips and, more importantly, if it can tug at the chords of fellow Malaysians and make them aware that we are, despite our various ethnic origins, really one people and one race, then I can say that it has been worthwhile.

ACKNOWLEDGEMENT

THIS book was born from a fruitful and enjoyable liaison with *The Star*, the leading English-language newspaper in Malaysia. In October 1993, I was invited by *The Star* to write a column for its Section 2. I decided to take up the challenge and write on things Malaysian as I felt that there was such a wealth of interesting material about Malaysians that was left largely unrecorded. The first article appeared on November 16, 1993. The column ran for two years and eight months. This book, *Malaysian Flavours*, is a compilation of articles from this column.

I would like to thank the great team at *The Star*—Steven Tan, the Managing Director, for his strong support; Ng Poh Tip, Group Chief Editor, who provided the impetus; Gilbert Yap, acting Editor of Section 2, who persuaded me to take on the role of newspaper columnist; and June H.L. Wong, Senior Editor of Section 2, for her encouragement throughout. I am also grateful to Lim Cheng Hoe, Lou Joon Yee, Johnni Wong and Julie Wong, who helped co-ordinate the column.

On the publication of this book, I would like to thank Ng Tieh Chuan, the Managing Director of Pelanduk Publications, for his belief in my book; and Eric C. Forbes, the Editor, for his patience and for being such a pleasure to work with.

To a dear friend, Harriet Wong, thank you for your wonderful enthusiasm. A note of thanks goes to Sermsuk Hussein, Low Kar Tiang, Dr Fong Tuck Choy, Patricia and Benny Loh, Loh Jun Jean, Lee Mee Ying, Fadillah Merican, Ruzy Suliza, and to friends, colleagues, relatives and students who provided comments, suggestions, or kind words of encouragement. My appreciation also goes to my sister, Su Win, and brother, Yu Ban. Lastly, thanks dear Jimmy, for your loving support and understanding, and Jan Ming, for being such an inspiration in my life.

CONTENTS

Preface
Acknowledgement

OBSERVATIONS

WORD FASHIONS

HIGHWAY HORRORS

MALAYSIAN NAMES

YESTERYEAR MEMORIES

MALAYSIAN ENGLISH

1. "SO HEATY-LAH!"
A light-hearted look
at Malaysian English

"*AIYAH, so heaty-lah! Afturds, my face break out in pimples, how?*"

"*You just had durians, now you wan coffee. Crazy-ah? Very heaty! Somemore today's weather so hot.*"

An English friend asked me the other day, "Just what does this word 'heaty' mean? Malaysians seem to use it so often." I was stumped. I had always assumed that it was part of the Queen's English. A furtive consultation with my trusty Oxford dictionary proved her right. There was no such word in the English language. Another favourite word with Malaysians is 'cooling'. While it does exist in English, its function is primarily in relation to time and objects such as 'a cooling-off period in industrial disputes' or 'a cooling tower'; and not so much for body functions. Malaysians, however, like to use it in the same way as 'heaty', such as:

"*Drink this soup. It's very cooling ... good for you.*"

Or "*Huh- You're pregnant-ah? Make sure you don't eat green bananas-hah. Very cooling ... no good for you.*"

These two words, 'heaty' and 'cooling', are used in Malaysian English, having been coined to suit our cultural and physiological needs.

One cannot help but be impressed at just how resourceful (or irreverent) Malaysians are in the usage of English. Familiar with a language from another culture but confronted with situations within our own culture, we have through the years nonchalantly coined Malaysian English words and phrases to fit the occasion.

3

The following is a list of words and phrases commonly used by Malaysians from all walks of life: call them colloquialisms, slang, jargon or Malaysianisms, they grow in number, changing through the times and have become quite entrenched in this vibrant nation's very own special brand of English.

1. Aiksy —to act in a conceited and arrogant manner. As in *"Wah ... so aiksy nowadays. Big shot already."*
2. Action —to show off. As in *"He got a new car. Action only ... drive around so fast."*
3. Die —used in almost any situation when one is in a spot. As in *"You die! You forgot her birthday!"*
    Or *"Aiiyaaah ... Die-lah, Die-lah. I'm late."*
    Or *"Die! Die! Die! I left my keys in the car!"*
4. Got —a verb used to substitute or eliminate all those nasty, tricky English verbs. As in *"I got so many problems-lah."*
    Or *"Where got time? Got three kids and a useless husband."*
    Or *"Where got? Where got? I never said that!"*
5. Your head —a direct translation from the Cantonese *lei keh tow!* which has got nothing to do with one's head but more so with what's inside. Used when scolding someone so usually implies that there's nothing inside one's head. As in *"Who said so? I never said that! Your head!"*
6. Friend you —to befriend someone. Very popular among kids. As in *"I doan friend you."*
7. One kind —unique, unusual, but with unflattering connotations. As in *"Her dressing ... one kind-lah."*
    Or *"She very one kind one-lah. Very hard to talk to her one."*
8. Gone case —a hopeless case, absolutely beyond help but used for rather trivial situations, certainly not in death or a case of going bananas. As in *"He-ah ... sure gone case-lah! Never study. How to pass?"*
9. Member —a friend. As in *"I don't want to go on the trip. No member."*

Or *"No shock-lah. My member not there."*

10. Shock — absolutely great, fabulous. Used for shock effect. As in *"I say, you must try the Curry Fishhead ... Shock only-lah!"*

11. Best — magnanimously used for everything that's superlatively good. As in *"How was the rock concert?" "Best".*
Or *"How's the food?" "Best".*

12. Tackle — to woo, to court a girl. As in *"Wah ... that girl ... so pretty. Must tackle-lah."*
Or *"Don't you dare tackle her. She's my sister."*

13. No problem — Malaysians' happy carefree answer when asked to do a favour. As in *"Can you help me-ah?" "No problem."*

14. Terror — used widely for anything or anybody that's unusual, difficult or strange. As in *"How was the exam?" "Terror-lah. Sure fail".*
Or *"Wah ... Terror-man! He got eight distinctions!"*

15. Kopi-oh license — used for very poor drivers. Implies that the driver has given some 'coffee' money (a bribe) in order to get the licence. As in *"Hei! What kind of driver-ah you?! Kopi-oh license ah?"*

16. Carry big leg — to curry favour with a particular person. Used by children and young people. As in *"He-ah ... so clever to carry Teacher's big leg. Hope Teacher will give him good marks ... Tink I donno-ah."*

17. Gostan — to reverse, probably a short form for 'to go astern'. As in *"Ei ... can please gostan a bit-ah? Your car blocking me-lah!"*

18. Outstation — to go out of town. Probably a colonial hangover from the days when the 'tuans' went up to the hillstations in Malaya for their vacations. As in *"My boss gone outstation awready ... That's why I enjoy. Shock only man!"*

19. Relek-*lah* — to relax, to take things easy, to have a good time. As in *"Relek-lah, Brudder!"*
Or *"What did you do during the holidays?" "Relek-lah".*

And finally, the famous *izzen it?*, Malaysians' answer to the difficult English Question Tag. In proper English, when the sentence is in the positive, then the question tag has to be in the negative, and vice versa, for example:

"You will write, won't you?"
"It wasn't that great, was it?"

In Malaysian English, that rule is happily dispensed away with; as in *"You're coming over with some durians, izzen it?"* and *"She's not in, izzen it?"*

And to conclude, *"You're fedup awready, izzen it?"*

2. THE IRREPRESSIBLE MALAYSIAN 'LAH'

IF you are strolling along the streets of London or sipping coffee at a sidewalk cafe somewhere in the heart of Paris, and you hear in plain English, "So expensive-*lah*" or "So hot-*lah*", just turn around in the direction where the voice came from and I guarantee you that ten out of ten, that person who just dotted his or her sentence with a *lah* is a Malaysian (or a Singaporean).

If you are feeling homesick in a foreign land and suddenly you overhear a conversation full of Yes-*lah*s and No-*lah*s, your homesickness can be assuaged for it sounds just like home and the speakers can only be Malaysians.

Just where did this *lah* come from and how did it creep into the English spoken by Malaysians? It is inevitable that Malaysians, living in a multilingual, multicultural setting will interborrow phrases and expressions from other languages. Thus, the very unique *lah*, used only in this part of the world, could have originated from Malay, or any of the local dialects or languages.

Only a Malaysian born and bred in this country will know how to use the *lah*. A Malaysian who has been away for a while can slip back into using it quite comfortably, but a Malaysian who has been away for a long time, say, seven to ten years, with little contact with fellow Malaysians, may find great difficulty as to exactly when to pepper his speech with *lah*. Just going *lah*, *lah*, *lah* every first or third word doesn't quite qualify. Malaysians will be able to sniff you out in a second and tell you that somehow, sorry-*lah*, you just don't make the grade. For example, try saying the following sentence aloud: "I-*lah* tell you-*lah* how-*lah* many times-*lah* but-*lah* you never-*lah* listen." Any true-blue

7

Malaysian will cringe and tell straightaway that any person who speaks like that is an impostor.

Foreigners newly arrived in Malaysia will find it quite baffling initially. Sure, these Malaysians are speaking English but what on earth is that strange musical note they place at the end of their sentences every so often? It does take some getting used to. Many foreigners have the mistaken notion that adding a *lah* to the end of every sentence lets them get away with a fairly good impression of a Malaysian accent. This is hardly the case. The use of *lah* is, in fact, quite an art for those who were not born into the language. Here are a few sophisticated variations of its use:

No fun-*lah*, you! (You're really no fun at all)
You see-*lah*, like that also you cannot do! (Can't you even do such a simple thing?)

What are the functions of the *lah*? What are the rules regarding its usage? How would you teach your *orang puteh* friend or spouse how to use the *lah* if he demands desperately for some help along the way? Well, I'm afraid one can't learn it formally. Like *sambal belacan* or *cincalok*, it's an acquired taste. You've got to be around for sometime, and gradually you'll acquire a taste for it.

If you think the *lah* is baffling enough as it is, Malaysians have more tail words up their sleeves or in this case, off their tongues. A great favourite is the *ah*, which has an entire repertoire of meanings, depending on how it is used. A simple "thank you" to a Malaysian may sound too curt and most Malaysians, in informal settings, would prefer to say "thank you-*ah*" as it sounds softer and friendlier. A "Yes-*lah*" and a "Yes-*ah*" response are also subtly different in meanings.

If someone were to ask you a question such as, "Are you coming along?", a "Yes-*ah*" response would be inappropriate whereas a "Yes-*lah*" response would be acceptable.

If your friend informed you that he's bought a brand new car, than a "Yes-*ah*" response would be fine, meaning "Oh really?" The "Yes-*ah*" could cover a whole gamut of responses ranging from being a question to a reply dripping in sarcasm depending on the intonation.

Another popular tail word is *one*, as in "I don't know what to say-*lah*. This kind of things very hard to say *one*" or "I'm so fed-up *one*, you know. I explain how many times in simple English, still cannot get through *one*."

Sometimes if you use *one* once too often, it can backfire. Your listener may find it hard to resist and may pun on your *one*. For example:

Lady: "I don't want *one*, but he wants so what can I do?"
Friend: "You don't want one *ah*, but you want two, yes or not?"

Yet another tail word is *man*, as in "I say, *man*. "Long time no see" or "I donno *man*". This is an interesting adaptation from American culture rather than an influence of the mother tongues. Malaysians can add *man* to any sentence arbitrarily and even to exclamations such as "Wah *man*! Solid."

To confuse things further, sometimes, Malaysians don't use single but double tail words at the end of a sentence, for example, "He's so *bodoh* (stupid) *one-lah*!" or "Why your dressing so Ah Beng *one-ah*?" And sometimes tail words do not appear at the end of sentences but somewhere in the middle, such as in sentences where the subject is delayed, for example: "So action *one man* he!" or "Terror *one-lah* she!"

Malaysians generally speak two types of English: proper English, particularly in business and professional settings, and Malaysian English, with its charming and unique expressions. Just as the French have their *oo-la-la*, the Italians their *Mama-mia*, and the English, endearing expressions like "By Jove" or "Well, jolly good", may our Malaysian *lah* live a long and healthy life! Say yes-*lah* to that!

3. JINJANG JOE
AND GANG

O VER the years, Malaysians have coined certain names and expressions to describe others based on their appearance, dressing or behaviour. These expressions are not malicious in intent but have been coined almost affectionately and playfully. The following are some of these names:

Jinjang Joe
A popular name back in the 1970s for a certain category of guys who liked to hang out particularly in shopping complexes such as Sungei Wang Plaza. Dressed in a *one kind* manner, usually high-waisted, broad-legged pants in dark shades of maroon or green, with large, loose shirts. Fond of wearing chunky heels and thick watch straps on wrists. Spoke mainly in Cantonese and particularly fond of emulating Hong Kong movie stars and singers in speech and mannerism. The first part of the name is named after a district called Jinjang in Selangor, while Joe is an American name, probably inspired by the American G.I. Joe!

Ah Pia
As in *"He's nice but aiyah, so ah pia!"* To look terribly 'square', a real old-fashioned stick-in-the-mud type, with hair cropped so short (usually by the Indian barber) that the stubble is still quite green. Most of the time out of sync with the rest of the crowd, and therefore may sometimes blurt out very refreshing, non-conformist opinions. Usually very brilliant, particularly in Mathematics, Calculus and Logic, but extremely blur in other departments, particularly the Social one.

During my campus days, Engineering students were fondly referred to as *Engine Ah Pias*. Whenever one of them tried to *tackle* a *woman* (the macho word for female undergraduate), they would be teased by their friends who would yell out loud, *"Hoi, Engine Ah Pia, stop 'smelling' around!"* ('Smelling' was the campus slang for wooing or chasing members of the opposite sex.)

Ah Beng
The Singapore equivalent to the Malaysian Ah Pia.

Auntie Auntie
As in *"You better change your wardrobe-lah! Your dressing look so auntie-auntie."* To look like an *Ah Soh*, an elderly Chinese auntie, fond of wearing westernised version of the Chinese *sam foo*, minus the Chinese collar, side opening and side slits, resulting in a mish-mash of neither *sam foo* nor pant suit. Entire pant suit is usually of polyester floral material in shades of browns, purples or greens, practical but certainly the most unexciting garb around. *Auntie-auntie* comes from the English word 'aunt' but is pronounced in a sing-song manner, à la Hong Kong style.

Mak Nenek
As in *"My third daughter is a real Mak nenek . . . loves to fuss over all of us."* To describe someone who has an extremely motherly disposition. Likes to mother her siblings and friends. Usually kind and unselfish although a bit of a fussbudget and a nag. Destined for the 'nurturing' professions such as nursing or teaching. *Mak* is the Malay word for 'mother' and *nenek* is the Malay word for 'grandmother'—imagine one's grandmother and mother packed into one!

Datin
As in *"Wah! Where do you think you're going? All dressed up, so datin-datin today!"* A fairly new expression on the scene. To describe someone dressed rather resplendently, not so much for work but for a grand social function. Usually in shiny shimmering silk, dripping with jewel-

lery or chunky accessories, a trend set by wealthy titled ladies around town. Shoes and bags should match (if shoes are orange, bag must be orange too, get it?) and hair has a well-sprayed, well-coiffured look. *Datin* is the female gender for *datuk*.

Cili Padi

As in *"His girlfriend-ah, ai say, real cili padi!" Or "I'm scared to talk to her-lah. She's the cili padi type."* Someone who looks like a real scorcher, flamboyant, sultry, sexy; or someone who possesses a fiery temper— once she loses her temper, nothing can save you! Interestingly, used only to describe females—as if males are such paragons of cool, controlled emotions. *Cili padi* is the Malay name for those tiny innocent-looking chillies, green or red in colour, usually found lurking in Malay and Peranakan dishes and floating about in Tom Yam soups. Try biting into one and you'll learn the instant meaning of how hot the word 'hot' can be, something which no English dictionary can ever get across!

4. NO HEAD, NO TAIL

IDIOMS are a colourful part of a language, and in a way, convey the flavour of a particular culture. When I was in school, we had to study whole lists of English idioms by heart. Some of them have become rather archaic while others are still in use today. The more outdated ones are proverbs such as 'make hay while the sun shines', and 'a stitch in time saves nine' probably because making hay and sewing aren't such common pastimes anymore.

I also enjoyed the idioms of the Malay language very much. We had a very strict Malay language teacher who made sure we knew the meanings of all the Malay idioms listed in the syllabus. She would write down six to ten idioms on the board each day which we then had to memorise like crazy. The next day, she would march into the class, while we shuddered and clattered, muttering the idioms under our breath. Pointing imperially at whoever caught her fancy, she would go, "You there—*bermula! Kaki Ayam?*" and the quaking student would have to stand up and give the meaning of *'Kaki Ayam'*. If anyone got stuck or fumbled, she would bark, machine gun-like "Next! Next!" Those who answered correctly got to sit down again while those who couldn't answer had to stand up. At the end of the 'test', the class looked like a battlefield with those who passed, almost passing out in relief over their desks, while those who couldn't answer correctly or on time, sticking up conspicuously like sore thumbs.

Who says rote-learning wasn't effective? Till today, I can still remember many of the more colourful *simpulan bahasa* and *perumpamaan*. Who can forget the dear *katak* (frog) under the *tempurung* (coconut shell), or the frightened *rusa* (deer) lost in the *kampung*, or the little mousedeer caught in the middle of the battle between elephants? Or the ungrateful peanut that *lupakan* (forgot) its *kulit* (skin)?

Today, there are quite a number of idioms being used quite non-chalantly in Malaysian English that actually do not exist in British and American English. This is because they are translations of the idioms of our various Malaysian dialects. Some of the more common ones are:

1. My ricebowl (my livelihood).
    Example: "Please help me pass this exam, it's my ricebowl, you know."
2. "I've tasted more salt than you." ("I'm more experienced than you"; or "I'm older and therefore have seen and gone through more of life than you.")
    Example: "Don't argue with me. I've tasted more salt than you."
3. Like a duck talking to a chicken (two persons talking to each other but on totally different wavelengths).
    Example: "So hard to talk to him, like a duck talking to a chicken."
4. Coffee money (under-counter money).
    Example: "Everything's gone up. Coffee money also has gone up!"
5. Shake legs (to have nothing much to do, to be quite free).
    Example: "His job is so easy, nothing to do but shake legs everyday."
6. Sour face (a dour expression on one's face).
    Example: "Next time, don't want to come here again ... look at the waitress, so sour face."
7. Half-past six (inadequate, just not competent).
    Example: "His work is one kind ... really half-past six."
8. New broom (from the Malay idiom *penyapu baru.* Someone new on the job who's all fired up with enthusiasm.)
    Example: "Just you wait and see. She's a new broom; a few more months, then you see-*lah* ...!"
9. No head, no tail (impossible to comprehend, nonsensical).
    Example: "I don't know what he's talking about ... no head, no tail!"

5. ON BEING COMPLIMENTED

HAVE you ever observed Malaysians when complimenting and accepting compliments? If you haven't, do so the next time. Keep your eyes and ears open and watch. More often than not, the response from the person being complimented is usually not a simple and straightforward 'thank you'!

The examples below are two actual instances of Malaysians responding to compliments:

Situation 1
At the Office
Colleague: Wah, Annie, you look very nice. I really like your dress!
Annie: No-*lah*, so old already this dress. I bought it at a sale. So cheap only ...

Situation 2
In a Shop
Friend A: You're so slim-hah! How do you keep so slim?
Friend B: No-*lah*, it's the dress. It's the cut; it hides my bulges well ....

Although we use English in much of our social interaction, our thought processes do not necessarily flow according to the culture of the language we operate in. Indeed, we are very much products of our own culture and the Malaysian way in accepting a compliment is usually a response that is modest, sometimes gently self-deprecatory, seldom in agreement with the compliment in a direct way.

We know that in the English language, the way to accept a compliment is to answer 'thank you'. Yet, for many of us, we somehow do not feel particularly comfortable responding in that manner. It is not because of a lack of sophistication or an excess of modesty. It is because in our cultures, we simply do not operate that way.

The usual way to respond to a compliment, Malaysian style, is to deflate it a little. Ways of responding can vary, but basically they can be divided into three types.

First, by softening the compliment, a technique of gently eroding a little bit off the whole impact of the compliment. For example:

A: Wah, you're looking so good nowadays.
B: No-*lah*, you mean I'm looking well-preserved.
Or
A: Your son so clever-*lah!* Eight distinctions in his SPM!
B: I think fluke shot-*lah*.

Second, by countering the compliment mildly or even vehemently disagreeing with the compliment. For example:

A: I like your hairstle. It looks great on you!
B: Yee! So curly-*lah!* I can't get used to it! Doesn't suit me.

Third, by giving background information. By deflecting the compliment a little by offering information even though the 'complimenter' never asked for it! For example:

A: What a beautiful dress!
B: I got it at this new place in town. Have you been there? Not bad you know the things there.

Sometimes, when a Malaysian is complimented, he or she can respond by complimenting right back in the very next breath, leaving the 'complimenter' having to figure out what to say, now that he or she has become the 'complimentee'! For example:

A: Wow, you look so lovely!

B: You also-*lah!* My, what a beautiful dress.

A: Er ... a bit tight round the waist-*lah* ... I'd better not eat so much afterwards.

At a regional seminar I attended several years ago, a foreigner, when presenting his paper, poked fun at Asians, saying how Asians just don't seem to be able to say 'thank you' when being complimented. His remark showed how little he understood of cultures and communication. It is not because we do not know how to say 'thank you' but because sometimes, we do not choose to.

The strategies we use do not mean that we do not know how to accept compliments or that we do not like being complimented. Who doesn't appreciate a sincere compliment coming along our way once in a while? The glow of appreciation and acceptance is there, unspoken. The need to express it does not override; it is understood. It is just that our way of responding may be a little different, and if you ask me, disarmingly charming.

6. THE MANY FACES OF 'FACE'

W HAT is 'face'? The dictionary meaning states that it refers to the front part of our head. But the other meaning of the word 'face' refers to that intangible something linked to our dignity, self-esteem and pride. Though the concept of 'face' is prevalent in Western as well as Eastern cultures, it is more predominant in Asian cultures.

'Face', to a large extent, governs our behaviour and interactions with one another. In Malaysia, preserving 'face' (*jaga maruah* in Malay or *lien mentzu* in Chinese) can be applied to all races. Malaysians generally refrain from criticising or embarrassing their peers in front of others as it would mean a loss of 'face'. Preserving 'face' is therefore an ongoing sensitivity, not taught consciously but culturally conditioned into us.

Expatriates working here may sometimes find this concept of 'face' perplexing and frustrating, particularly at the workplace. Why all this face-saving? Why can't they be frank and open? Why all this indirectness and obliqueness? I guess it's a matter of priorities. Frankness is a quality that is much valued and admired, but if because of frankness, 'face' is lost, resulting in disharmony and strained interpersonal relationships, then frankness should be suspended for the sake of 'face'.

Many expressions with regard to one's face has crept into our brand of Malaysian English. For instance, the expression 'to give face' means not to affront someone by being gracious to that person. Example: "Even if you don't want to go to the function, you have to go. You must give face a bit." Or, "Next time, if he talks to you like that, ignore him! Don't give him face!"

The expression 'to save face' is to preserve one's or someone else's dignity. Example: "Actually, he never completed his portion of the work, but we covered up for him. Save his face for him."

'To lose face' is to lose one's dignity or pride. Example: "You know what happened or not? I tripped and fell in front of everybody! So shameful-*lah!* Lose face only."

'To show face' is from the Malay idiom *menunjuk muka*. It literally means to show face at, or to attend a function for a brief period of time. However, it also has some connotations of 'giving face' to the host by attending the function, and 'saving face' if one is expected to attend. Example: "I know you're dead tired but we still have to go to the dinner. Just show face for a short while-*lah*."

Face is pervasive in Asia. In Japan, even if you are not in the wrong and the other person is, it helps your case to apologise. This helps to save face all round. For instance, a wife went to visit her husband who was working in Japan on a short stint. On her arrival, she learnt that her luggage had been misplaced by the Japanese authorities. The Japanese asked her to apologise, to which she adamantly refused as it was not her fault that her luggage was lost. Her husband persuaded her to apologise. She reluctantly agreed feeling very unhappy about having to do so, and was amazed to find that matters were expedited and she got her luggage back very quickly, without too much shame on the part of the Japanese for having made a mistake.

In Hong Kong, when a Chinese businessman gives you his word, it is as good as a legal document. If he goes back on his word, then he loses face, which implies bringing shame on himself and on his family. The Thais do not like to say 'no' when a request is made of them. They are a gentle and gracious people, and having to say 'no' implies a loss of face for the person making the request. Therefore instead of an outright 'no', a gently indirect answer is usually the norm.

There are also degrees of 'face'. Some cultures value 'face' more intensely than others even within a totally Asian setup. For persons working in a multi-cultural setting, it helps to be aware of the concept of preserving face. Therefore, 'face' is not a bad thing if you think about it. It cuts down on open confrontation, public embarrassment and humiliation. Its objective is harmony, even if it's only on the surface.

7. ON THE FAN, PLEASE!

SOMEDAY, sometime, someone might say this to you: *"On the fan, please."* If you're a Malaysian, you'll probably know exactly what it means. If you're a foreigner, however, permit me to explain. It is not a request for you to climb onto the fan. It is simply a request for you to switch on the fan! Tardiness, laziness, expediency ... who knows? Somewhere along the way, in Malaysian English, the poor verbs 'switch' and 'turn' have been dropped and instead the prepositions 'on' and 'off' have taken on the job.

"Hoi! Off the volume-lah! I can't hear myself speak!" This was heard over the radio in one of those phone-in talk shows. The young lady, who had just phoned in, was trying to conduct a conversation with the deejay of the show, but had great difficulty because of the noise from her radio. Suddenly, the whole nation could hear her hollering to her sister in the background to *'off the volume-lah!'*

What are prepositions? Prepositions are nifty little signal words that are used to express relationships pertaining to space, time, etc. They have objects, normally nouns and pronouns and there are certain rules governing their usage. Prepositions also contain specific meanings depending on how they are used: "My boss looked at me" would certainly have quite a different meaning from "My boss looked through me". Whatever the rule, there is certainly no rule that allows you to drop the verb altogether and have the preposition carry out the function of the verb. However, in Manglish (namely, Malaysian English), the two prepositions 'on' and 'off' have been beautifully mangled, and it's quite possible for you to be perfectly understood, even in highly educated circles, without raising even the flicker of an eyebrow when you go, *"Can you please on the light for me-ah?"* or *"Off the air-con"* or *"On the tap, please"*.

23

The pronunciation of 'on' and 'off' when used in this way is slightly different from the way they are pronounced as ordinary prepositions. The syllables are dragged out a little longer and pronounced with much more emphasis and authority. After all, the little preposition has been promoted to the rank of the verb and surely needs all the clout it can get!

Prepositions may look quite harmless, but if used in the wrong context, can cause quite a flutter. An elderly aunt of mine was travelling to Kuala Lumpur by plane. She never did like travelling by plane much. The last part of the journey had been rough and bumpy, and she was feeling jittery. As the plane approached Subang International Airport, suddenly, over the intercom came a solemn message from the pilot.

"Ladies and Gentlemen, I have an announcement to make. We are going down now."

The poor lady almost died of shock. With her good command of English, she of course assumed that 'going down' when announced on board a plane meant that they were going to crash! What the pilot should have said was, "We are going to land now", and not "We are going down now"!

Talk about 'if looks can kill', looks like words can too.

8. EXCLAMATIONS, MALAYSIAN-STYLE

WHEN the English wish to exclaim their astonishment, dismay, disgust, they have their special expressions ranging from "Oh my goodness", "Goodness gracious", "Oh dear" and "Oh dear me" to "By jove" and "Blimey". The Americans too have their own range of expressions such as "Gosh", "Damn it", "What the heck" and "Great balls of fire". Of course, as with all languages, there are many more exclamatory expressions which I've left out because they are unprintable, irreverent or downright rude.

Malaysia, being a melting-pot of so many cultures, has an incredible array of exclamations as well, ranging from the acceptable cute phrases, widely used by all communities, to the unmentionables. Below are just some of the more commonly used stock expressions that Malaysians like to use:

1. *Alamak!* This is a popular expression used by all races. It is used to express surprise, for example, "Alamak! You gave me the shock of my life. Next time, knock first before you enter, will you!" Also used when one wishes to express dismay. The "mak" is sometimes stretched out a little longer from the "ala-mak" used to denote surprise, such as: "Alamaa-aak! I went and called my boss' wife the wrong name!" Or "Alamaa-aak! I forgot to fetch my wife from the airport!"

2. *Amboi!* Used to tease a person, usually in a mild and playful manner. Of Malay origin, it can also be applied scathingly if one so wishes. For example, "Amboi! So *sombong* (proud) nowadays, some people ..." Or "Amboi! *Bukan main cantiknya!* (so beautiful!) Dressed to kill-ah today?"

25

3. *Adoi!* Also of Malay origin, used to express pain, similar to the English "Ouch!" For example, "Adoi! Painful one, you know! Why you pinch me like that?!" Sometimes also used even when there's no pain inflicted. For example, if a gorgeous girl walks past a group of young men hanging about, these young men, with a surfeit of male hormones, go "Adoooooiii ...!", expressed with breathless ardour. No pain inflicted except on the hormones and definitely a throbbing heart!

4. *Wah!* Used to express surprise, amazement, appreciation. Of Malay origin. For example: "Wah! Her house-ah, so grand one. Big semi-dee, you know. Got electronic gate. Some more-ah got marble flooring, you know! I'm so jealous. My floor only terrazzo!"

5. *Cheh!* Used to express disgust, disappointment. Of Chinese origin. For example: "Cheh! You call this *teh tarik*-ah? No froth at all!"

6. *Choy!* A Cantonese exclamation expressed to ward off bad luck. It is believed that if you say *Choy!* loudly when something unlucky has been spoken, the bad luck will hopefully be deflected. For example: "Choy! Choy! Stop saying die! will you? Today is Chinese New Year, you know ... bring bad luck only!"

7. *Aiyo!* To express concern, dismay, surprise. Probably derived from the Tamil exclamation *Aiyoyo!* but there is no empirical evidence to support this statement. For example: "Aiyo! How-ah? I haven't passed up my work!"

8. *Aiya!* Similar to *Aiyo!*

When I was a little girl, my father used to drive us around in his car, an old Hillman. Whenever he got caught in an exasperating traffic situation or encountered an obnoxious driver cutting into his lane, he would swear to give vent to his frustration by muttering "Barsket!"

And when really mad, he'd go "Bladibarsket!" I used to wonder why Papa had such a funny way of swearing—calling upon a totally mundane object.

It was only much later that I learnt that "Barsket" was Papa's (and indeed quite a number of Malaysians of his time) way of expressing something unmentionable, especially in front of the children, yet allowed him the pleasure of giving vent to his frustration and anger. "Barsket" was the 'euphemism' for 'bastard'.

9. TWISTING THE ENGLISH TONGUE

AT the end of a visit to the home of two friends of mine, an English couple, I found myself saying: "Okay, it's getting late. I really must make a move now."

Peter, the Englishman, teased me and said: "What's this move you're going to make?"

Of course, what I meant was that I planned to "make a move to go home" but if you check with a native speaker of the English language, it's not very commonly used. The English don't usually say "make a move" when they are going to take leave. They might use it when playing a game of chess perhaps, or when planning to take a course of action.

However, the phrase is quite common among Malaysians. It is a colloquial expression found in Malaysian as well as Singaporean English. We use colloquialisms so often that we assume they are part of the English language, but try using them with a native speaker and you might get strange looks.

The following are more Malaysian colloquialisms.

"Please pass up your work."
Teacher says: "Please pass up your work." ("Pass up" is usually pronounced as "parsup".)

Students say: "Norchet, Teacher." ("Norchet" is a lazily pronounced version of "not yet".)

"Pass up your work, essays or assignments" is very commonly used by Malaysians, but in fact, is not altogether correct. It should instead be: "Please hand in your work."

"I'll send you to the airport."

"I'll send you to the airport" is another colloquialism. To a foreigner, it sounds as if you are going to put him in an envelope, seal it, paste a stamp on it, and drop him off at the nearest post-box!

When you send someone or something away, you don't go along with the object or the person; for example, you send a letter or you send the pesky salesman away. But, ah well, I can understand how this one evolved in Malaysian English. It is so much more apt and graphic. Why should it be confined to letters, parcels and the postal system? How can we resist using it to 'send the kids to tuition classes', 'send So-and-So to the airport', and 'send Mother-in-law home'?

"Eh, can you fetch me home from work today, ah?"

"Okay, I must make a move now. I'm late. I've got to fetch my kids from school." One fetches water from the well, or you command the dog to fetch the stick. "Fetch" is a verb which means "to get something, usually an inanimate object".

But then, like "send", it does seem such a convenient verb to use. "Eh, can you fetch me home from work today, ah?" gets the message across so much more succinctly, wouldn't you agree? (Though "please pick me up" and "drive me home" are the correct phrases to use.)

"Follow Joe's car!"

A dialogue overheard after a party.

The hostess says, "I'll send you home, Nora, as your house is nearby only. But Sue, you follow Joe, okay, since you both live in Bangsar. Who else is from Bangsar? Follow Joe's car!"

Now, if the guests who live in Bangsar take their hostess' advice literally, there would be a group of people trailing *behind* Joe's car, and not *in* it! For that's the meaning of "follow". However, Malaysians know that when "follow" is used in this context, it means "to accompany or to go along with".

"My off-day is tomorrow, not today."

A says: "Hey? How come you're here today? I thought it's your off-day today." B replies: "No-*lah*. My off-day is tomorrow, not today."

An "off-day", correctly speaking, means taking a day off because one is not feeling well, but with Malaysians, it simply means a day off from work. So when Malaysians say it's their off-day, it hardly means that they are feeling sick or down, but most likely the reverse is true!

"Can, can."
Friend: "Eh, Chong, can I borrow your phone, ah?"
Chong: "Can, can!"
Or,
Tan: Where's your phone? I need to make a call, can or not?
Lee: "Can, can."

The correct response would be "yes" and not "can". "Can" is actually a modal, a part of speech used to indicate permission or ability. Malaysians are very fond of it though and if you don't believe me, just go out there and listen to the way we speak and you'll hear this "can-can" quite often.

It could be because of the influence of our own tongues and dialects; for example, the Malay *boleh, boleh*, the Cantonese *tuck, tuck,* or the Hokkien *eh sai, eh sai*, all of which are equivalent to the concept of "can".

A colleague from Holland told me she found the way Malaysians go "can, can" quite charming and something that she would always remember and associate with her visit to this country.

When I agreed that, yes, it really is quite quaint, a colleague from Canada warned me about the dangers of using the word 'quaint', that its meaning had changed from its original one to something more off-colour! Say what?! I'll have to check on that!

ALAMAK! BLOOPERS AND BOO-BOOS

10. ENGLISH IS ALIVE AND IN THE WELL

YES, I know, I know, we've heard it often enough. English is on the decline. The standard of English is falling. English is going to the dogs in this country. And yes, we've got to do something about it. We've got to arrest it. We've got to bring back Grammar. We're going to end up speaking Pidgin English. Yes, yes, we've heard that too.

Well, have I got an answer? I'm afraid not. In fact, my intention here is to add more fat to the fire. Teaching English is a very difficult task. We've got to make sure that our students achieve communicative competence. Not only do we have to ensure that they master grammatical competence and discourse competence but there's another kind of competence that they've got to acquire as well—sort of the icing on the cake—and that is, sociolinguistic competence.

What is this thing called sociolinguistic competence? Put simply, it means having a knowledge of the rules of appropriateness when using language in different social contexts.

There was a time when students, if they spoke English correctly, innately knew what manner to speak it, what kind of tone and nuances to use, and understood perfectly the sociolinguistic context in which the speech act was taking place. However, it is not uncommon today to come across users of English who are able to speak and write grammatically correct English, but are sociolinguistically incorrect. Let us look at some examples:

Example 1
A note from a student to a lecturer reads: "I was not able to see you today. I shall see you tomorrow at 10.30a.m."

Example 2
An invitation from students to lecturers reads: "You are invited to our gathering which will be held on June 9. Make sure that all of you come in order to make it a success."

Example 3
Knock, knock.
Teacher: Yes, Come in.
Student: Aaaa ... Miss, Miss, I want to see you.

Are there any grammatical errors in these examples? None whatsoever. Has the message been communicated? Yes, but along with it, the person has also communicated, unintentionally, an underlying message which may range from rudeness to sheer presumptuousness.

In Example 1, the student does not seem to know the conventions of making appointments, particularly in a semi-formal or formal relationship between student and teacher. He gets his message across but also ends up annoying his teacher with his high-handed manner.

In Example 2, the person being invited is made to feel that he is being invited not for his presence at the function but for the sole purpose of making the event a success, which probably is the truth, and yet sounds awkward when phrased in such a direct manner.

Example 3 sounds rude and offensive. Many students are unaware that calling a lady teacher 'Miss' without her name attached to it is impolite (whereas addressing a male teacher 'Sir' sounds fine).

Such instances as those above are perfectly understandable today as English is a second language. Just mastering the grammatical system is a feat in itself, what more the social niceties. Some have argued that it doesn't really matter as long as one gets the message across. But my argument is wouldn't it be much more effective if one gets the message across effectively? What a waste to hear good English going to waste— sort of like half-finished Eliza Doolittles, requiring a little more polish before going to the Ball.

Native language interference can also pose a problem. The other day, my phone rang and the woman at the end of the line stumped me with this question, "Hello. Is this a house?" This was a direct translation from a local Chinese dialect. Not wanting to appear rude nor embarrass her, I found myself answering, "Er ... yes. This is a house ..." Who was I to start explaining the subtle difference between "this is a house" and "this is a private residence", I thought. Anyway, the woman put the phone down feeling quite satisfied (that she'd got the wrong number), and I put down my phone feeling quite stupid—if I had been a house, I wouldn't have been able to reply!

The other classic example of direct translation is this introduction in a letter which I received—"Dear Teacher, I am in the well. I hope you are in the well too ..." (a direct translation from the Malay, *"saya didalam keadaan sihat. Saya harap cikgu didalam keadaan sihat juga"*)—which made me feel quite unwell. Another example which a colleague shared with me was this incident which occurred at the end of the semester. This particular colleague was a distinguished-looking gentleman, a senior citizen with silver hair. As he bade his students farewell, one student came up to him, shook his hand and with the best of intentions, respectfully said, "Sir, I wish to pay my last respects to you!"

Sometimes, teaching one's students to use the dictionary may not solve one's lexical problems that simply, as in this conclusion of a letter a student wrote, "I must *terminate* now. My friend, please reply soon". Or, even worse, this sentence in a composition about the buildings on campus, "The greatest *erection* on this campus is the Great Hall"!

So, yes, there's no doubt about it. English is definitely on the decline. When students tell you that there's a typographical error when they come across a sentence like "She had had her dinner when the fire broke out" then, you know that the Past Perfect Tense has seen more perfect days in the past. So, I too shall ask the oft-asked question: isn't it about time we did something serious to stop the rot? Otherwise, we risk producing a generation of rude, obnoxious-sounding speakers of English.

Or potential disasters as in this case in point. A passenger was very pleased with the excellent service he received in the Business Class section of a certain airline, until the air stewardess opened her mouth. She had just placed in front of him a delicious serving of meatballs. Then, smiling graciously, with a sauce jar in her hand, she asked in earnest innocence, "Sir, would you like some sauce on your balls?" to which he sternly replied, "I most certainly would not!" and so never quite got to enjoy the Meatballs.

11. ALAMAK!

I guess we all have, some time or other, been involved in a blunder or two as we plod along our respective journeys through life. Some of us are incorrigible bunglers, losing things such as contact lenses, keys and sunglasses. There are others amongst us who, if there are things to trip over, will trip over them and so you'll see these characters tripping over carpets, wires, falling off steps, bumping into bins. And there are those who say the wrong things at the wrong time.

Even presidential figures are not spared the occasional blunder. Remember the famous boo-boo by Dan Quayle, the former Vice-President of the United States? His attempt at correcting a little boy's spelling of the plural tense of the word 'potato' from 'potatoes' to 'potatos' was publicised throughout the world! Ronald Reagan, the former President of the United States, was so overwhelmed by the presence of the beautiful Diana, Princess of Wales, that in his welcoming speech to the British royal couple, he quite forgot to welcome Prince Charles during the couple's visit to the United States!

Of course there are those who never ever slip, who are always in control, never a sync out of step. On the whole, however, most of us have a pet blunder or two which with the passing of Time we may enjoy recapitulating with our friends.

An expatriate friend, Bob, likes to tell this story of what happened to him when he first came to Malaysia. Bob had just arrived from Australia to work for a multinational company in the Golden Triangle district of Kuala Lumpur. One day, his car broke down right in the middle of town. He called his colleague, Tom, also an expatriate, for help from a public telephone. When Tom asked him where he was, Bob said, "I'm at Jalan Sehala."

"What?"

"I said I'm at Jalan Sehala. Could you please get here fast? It's darn hot."

Tom asked, "Jalan Sehala? Are you sure you're at Jalan Sehala? I don't remember any such road in this area with such a name."

"Well, you bet I'm sure. There's a signboard right here that says Jalan Sehala ... now if that's not the name of a road, then what the heck is it?"

"Alright, alright, I'll come and get you," said Tom.

Tom never managed to find Bob that day. Can't really blame the poor guy ... After all, there are so many 'Jalan Sehalas' (Malay phrase for one-way street) in town! Perhaps it's time we made our signboards more foreigner-friendly. I worry about poor Bob's car breaking down yet again at 'Jalan Tutup' ('Road is Closed') or 'Jalan Mati' ('Dead End')!

On our first trip to the East Coast many years ago, my girlfriends and I went shopping at the Kuala Trengganu market. On the first floor of the market was a bewildering array of goods such as batik, baskets, *keropok, mengkuang* mats, etc. My friend Liza wanted to try on a flimsy rayon batik blouse. As there were no changing rooms, she just slipped on the blouse to try it for size. It was a blouse with no buttons or zips, so all one had to do was to slip it over one's head.

When she took off the blouse she accidentally lifted in one flourish her own blouse as well. We all stared at her with our mouths slowly opening, slow-motion style, in frozen disbelief. Why was our friend standing there in the middle of a marketplace without her clothes on? Liza did not realise her stripshow act at first ... then, she stiffened ... perhaps she felt a draught or saw our gaping expressions. She looked down and "Aieeee- eee!"—we all screamed at the same time which attracted even more attention! The *mak cik* sitting nearby quickly threw a sarong over her. Thus, began and ended Liza's short career as a female flasher!

I made a boo-boo once. Deep in the pristine rainforests of Malaya. It was on a trip to Taman Negara organised by the Malaysian Nature Society. With a group of scientists and some society members, we trekked along the jungle path to a beautiful stream.

Said one scientist to another, "I saw a pig-tailed macaque on the way here."

I was standing nearby, and with a totally different frame of reference operating in my head, I opened my big mouth and said, "Oohhhhh .... Really? Did it really have pig tails?"

In my mind, I envisaged a cute little monkey whose hair had been tied into little pigtails by its mother. After all, from what I remember of childhood trips to the zoo, the monkeys—whether macaques, baboons or chimpanzees—were forever preening themselves and rummaging amongst each other's hair for *kutu* (ticks). How was I to know that monkeys haven't progressed since then?

The two scientists gaped, wondering if I was being facetious or serious. *Alamak!!* It dawned on me there and then that they were actually talking about, well, about pig-tailed macaques, a common species of monkeys whose names are derived from their little twirly piglike tails. I quickly tossed back my head and laughed deliriously as if terribly impressed by my own wit, then toddled into the stream, wishing that it would wash me away. I wonder if the two scientists found me out.

Still, whenever I go into the rainforests, I can't help looking at the trees and scanning the branches. Who knows? Perhaps one day I will see a pig-tailed macaque—MY version, and not the official, scientific one.

12. SIGN LANGUAGE

IF ever you are travelling as a passenger on a journey through Malaysia and are feeling bored, one way of entertaining yourself is to look at the Boards that pass you by ... no, not at fellow Boreds like yourself but at the signboards that are placed in front of shops, coffeeshops, restaurants and along roads and streets. They can be quite entertaining.

Take this signboard which I saw in the midst of some bushes along a road off Jalan Ampang. It said 'Body Beating Service Here'. I was intrigued. What on earth did it mean? Was it advertising a massage service using plummelling techniques or was it some kind of Mafia joint where you could hire somebody to beat up another body? Or was it a meeting place for pain-loving perverts? A glance around the area behind the bushes and my wild flights of imagination were somewhat stifled. There, beyond the bushes stood a rather beaten-up, dilapidated workshop and in it were two beaten-up cars, and a few more battered-looking vehicles in the vicinity. There were also some scruffy-looking fellows with hammers in their hands beating the cars, probably victims of accidents (the cars, not the fellows), back into shape. It was a workshop where for a fee, the bodies of cars were beaten back into their original form and made to look as good as new.

Another signboard which I came across was this—'Do Not Enter. Trespassers Will Be Executed' accompanied by a picture of a figure holding a gun as if about to shoot. Now, this was serious business. Correct me if I'm wrong but surely the standard cliché for such signboards is 'Trespassers will be Prosecuted', and not 'Executed'. Still, my intuition told me that this was no place to act cute and to try and find out whether the owner had gotten his verbs mixed up, and so I got out fast, and thankfully, lived to see another day.

If you're travelling up to Genting Highlands, you'll pass a Chinese temple to your right, halfway up the mountain. Slow down a little and you'll see an eye-catching sign outside the temple. It says, 'Vegetarian Available Here.' It sounds as if some monk or nun has gotten lonely ... but in actual fact, the word 'Food' has been left out, an omission error which I hope has got nothing to do with eating too much vegetables.

On the way to Bangi, there was once a sign advertising country living. I'm sure you've seen quite a number of these advertisements around ... you know, those advertising Country Homes, the latest fad in genteel living. It's strange how the more Nature is cleared to make way for these homes, the more rapturous the adverts get about living in the midst of Nature. The sign read, 'Country Homes—Experience the Germs of a Lifetime'! What a gem—it has caused many a traveller's heart to lift in humour and many a mouth to twitch with laughter. However, the signboard has been removed ... perhaps, for fear that the germs might spread.

In a housing estate in Petaling Jaya, a tailor whose business grew to a size she couldn't handle decided to advertise for an assistant. This was the sign she placed outside her house: 'Sewer Wanted'. I wonder what the response was like.

Driving around the Bukit Bintang-Jalan Imbi area in Kuala Lumpur one day, a friend of mine from Switzerland was intrigued by a signboard he saw outside a clinic. The words on the signboard were 'Chin Ear Nose Throat Clinic'. I guess the fact that my friend was a chiropractor by profession had something to do with his interest in body parts. Anyway, he asked, "I know one can specialise in the ear, nose and throat ... but how does one specialise in the chin?" My friends and I squealed with laughter which shocked him even further for in Switzerland, according to him, laughter is conducted as quietly as possible. We explained to him that Chin was the surname of the Ear Nose Throat doctor of that particular clinic, and was not a part of the human anatomy. Thinking back over that incident, I can't help musing over how nice it would be if one day, we actually had chin clinics. People who are unhappy with their chins could just walk in and have a chin job done. I can imagine the conversation going something like this: "Excuse me, doctor, I'd like you to alter my chin—it doesn't quite match my nose."

Or says Patient: "I'm really depressed, Doc. I've got a sunken chin. Could you elevate it a little?" Says Doctor: "No problem. I'll up your chin in no time, so chin up, my dear."

Why, chins might just be the rage.

13. SNAKES AND REINDEER

THERE'S an old English proverb that says, "A little knowledge is dangerous". This is particularly so when learning a language. When we learn a language as a second or a foreign language, we usually learn it in its safe, sanitised version, usually the formal standard register. But a language is of course much more complex than that. It also has its sub-registers, its metaphors and idiomatic expressions, its colloquialisms, etc. Therefore, one has to tread carefully if unfamiliar with the language. For some languages in particular, say it just a little off-key and you might find yourself being given strange looks.

Once, I set an English composition task where the students had to write a story based on a series of pictures. The pictures showed two friends going on a jungle expedition. Along the way, one of them was bitten by a snake. The other continued his journey and eventually found some buried treasure. The composition was quite satisfactorily written until the part where the two men were attacked by the snake. The student wrote this sentence to describe what happened: 'Suddenly, the snake bit his member off'! 'Member' is Malaysian English slang for 'friend' and the student's intention was to state that the snake had killed off the protagonist's friend. However, what resulted certainly was not what my student had intended.

Discreetly, I crossed out the offending word 'member' and wrote in the margin that the correct word should be 'friend'. But I confess that that was all I did. I certainly was not about to explain to the young man that he had just 'dismembered' the main character of his story, or that his snake had just done a Lorena Bobbit on the poor jungle explorer. Still, I couldn't resist writing in the margin (beside the part lamenting the death of the friend)—"and so, we have to 're-member' him". Alas, my pun was quite lost on the student.

Another example is this amusing incident narrated to me by a friend, Basil. In this example, it was not a case of using a wrong word but a case of totally not being aware of the sub-registers and sub-cultures of the English language. Basil was studying abroad in the United States. One day, while browsing in a bookshop, he bumped into a friend, a young Russian girl, newly-arrived in the United States for further studies. She was not very proficient in the English language but managed. She was shopping around for a Christmas card to give to her boyfriend, an American whom she had recently met. Finally, she found one which she liked a lot. Just before she left the shop, she showed Basil the card. On the front of the card was a magnificent reindeer with the finest set of antlers one had ever seen. There was tinsel everywhere and the card looked really pretty. Basil took a peek at the inside of the card. The message written inside was something else! It said: 'From One Horny Person to Another!'

Basil did not know her well enough to make any assumptions or to explain that 'horny' did not just refer to reindeer in their prime. And so, he confessed that he too left the matter at that. One can only wonder how the recipient of the card reacted.

14. WHEN THE WAITER CAME ALONG

HAVE you heard the new commercial aired over Radio 4 recently? It is delightful, and wickedly funny. It is about this gauche lady trying very hard to acquire some airs and to be 'seen' with genteel society, the sort who have nothing much to do but have afternoon tea amidst elegant surroundings at elegant hotels.

This lady speaks with a really strong Chinese accent. She meets an acquaintance (a sophisticated, snobbish type who tries to speak with a heavy British-English accent) and gushes over how glad she is to have been introduced to the word 'scones' for she now simply enjoys having English afternoon teas at the hotel's lobby lounge. Then she summons the waitress and orders her favourite scones, finger sandwiches, croissants—all pronounced extremely badly. When the waitress asks the lady what kind of tea she would like, "Darjeeling or Earl Grey?", she replies affectedly, " Er ... just tea please" not realising that Darjeeling and Earl Grey are the names of different types of teas!

This reminds me of an incident back in my undergraduate days. A friend of mine had just graduated with an engineering degree and was looking for a job. He was shortlisted by a prestigious multinational company and managed to pass a series of interviews. Then came the final interview and test. He and another candidate had to go for lunch with the managers. He thought he performed rather well at the lunch, a formal Western affair. He used the cutlery correctly, tried not to slurp his soup and made sure he did not order anything that required major wrestling and dissection with the knife and fork.

Then along came the waiter to take their orders for coffee. The waiter asked my friend, "And how would you like your coffee, sir, black or white?"

My friend was stumped! All his life, his only experience with coffee was the coffee that came out of his mother's coffee pot. She certainly did not have the time nor the inclination to ask him about his colour preferences. And throughout varsity days, nobody asked you about your coffee either—the coffee came in weak bland shades and tasted either disgustingly sweet or as tasteless as drainwater.

The waiter saw the blank look on my friend's face and tried to cue him. "With sugar or milk, Sir?" Aha! So that was it! my friend thought. He told the waiter, as everyone listened intently, "Black, please, with milk"!

Whether it was because of the coffee boo-boo or not, he never quite found out; but he didn't get the job.

I am reminded of another incident also pertaining to Western meals and placing orders. A relative of mine, young, naive and unexposed, having grown up in a small town in Malaysia, came to the big city of KL to work. He got a job with a big electronics company. One day, he went out for lunch with his colleagues. He ordered what his colleagues were ordering: Sizzling Steak. The waiter asked him, "How would you like it done, Sir?"

He was stumped. Then he vaguely remembered something he had heard others use before, something that started with the letter 'R'. So he told the waiter, "Raw, please"! The waiter walked away calmly and came back later with a steak that was done, rare, and not as ordered—raw!

How these waiters keep such straight expressions on their faces, I'll never know.

CROSS-CULTURAL ENCOUNTERS

15. WHERE ARE YOU GOING? HAVE YOU EATEN?

CROSS-cultural encounters occur when a person nurtured by one culture is placed in juxtaposition with another and an interaction of some sort takes place. If a misunderstanding occurs because of a cross-cultural encounter, it is important to remember that the miscommunication was not borne out of an intention to offend by any party, but because of a difference in ideas, attitudes or behaviour which are culture-based. A cross-cultural encounter may be one of curiosity, delight, enchantment, or on the negative side, confusion, anxiety or fear.

An American professor on his first teaching stint to this country got rather nervous and irritated during his stay here. He complained that every morning as he stepped out of his condominium apartment and headed for the lift, the security guard on that particular floor would ask him in English, "Where are you going?" The professor would reply, "I'm going to work" and this would take place every time they met. This resulted in the professor feeling very agitated at what seemed to him like a daily interrogation, and an intrusion into his private life. Besides, to the professor's mind, the guard was supposed to query strangers and not residents of the apartment.

Only after it was explained to the professor that the guard, a Malay, was just trying to be friendly, in a way in which he was familiar with, was the professor relieved of his anxieties. *"Pergi mana?"* or *"Nak pergi mana?"* (the literal translation in English is 'Where are you going?') is a Malay form of greeting and does not require one to give an exact answer. It is a common practice in Malaysia even amongst the other races when greeting someone and does not imply any kind of intrusiveness into one's private affairs. *'Pergi mana?'* sounds so gentle and friendly when spoken in its lilting native form but when translated into English may come across as rude and direct to foreigners, especially Westerners who value privacy. Malaysians, however, are quite used to it and understand its context perfectly even if the question is posed to them in English.

The Chinese too have a greeting which is in the form of a question. This is *'Sek pau mei?'* in Cantonese or *'Chiak pa boei?'* in Hokkien. It literally means 'Have you eaten till full?' and like *'Pergi mana?'* does not expect one to give an accurate answer. The Chinese have a great love for food and it does seem quite natural that the greeting form should reflect this. Likewise, the Malay greeting *'Apa Khabar?'* ('What's the news?'), which is of Arabic origin, does not expect one to come out with a detailed account of one's current affairs. A simple reply of *'Khabar baik'* ('The news is good') would suffice.

A cross-cultural encounter which I found quite charming occurred when my husband and I were in Club Med in Cherating. We sat down to dinner with another Malaysian couple and two Japanese couples, probably honeymooners. When the first course was brought to our table, the two Malaysian gentlemen took it upon themselves to dish out the soup for the rest of us. It was an interesting moment for at the same time, the two young Japanese wives were just about to do the same. In Japanese culture the women are tradition-bound to serve their husbands. Instead, they found themselves being served by the two Malaysian men. They blushed and looked flustered and yet pleasantly surprised. The two Japanese men looked uncomfortable at being served by the other men and not by their wives.

I was intrigued by the situation. Who would serve the next course? Would it be the Japanese women (to show that they haven't forgotten their customs) or should it be the Malaysian women (to show that we also serve our menfolk) or should we allow the two Malaysian men to serve us again (to show that it's really nice for such gallantries especially in such a lovely and romantic setting?) It was indeed getting quite complicated and I sat with bated breath waiting for the next course, hoping that it was 'serveable' and that the waiter wouldn't spoil it all by serving the food himself. When the next course arrived, fortunately, the waiter had to move along to the next table. The dish had to be portioned out. Here was the moment I had been waiting for—Who was to serve next? Which culture or gender would prevail? Whose instincts would overcome the rest?

What transpired was something I had not expected—the two Japanese men, looking a little abashed, stood up and served us all! I was taken by surprise for in the culture of the Japanese, women serve their men and not the other way around. Here were two Japanese men who were able to transcend their cultural boundaries and rise to the spirit of the occasion. But of course, the most surprised and thrilled that night were the two Japanese wives who blushed again and appeared even more flustered this time around.

Cross-cultural encounters need not have to happen only between people of different nationalities. It could also happen across different ethnic groups or even across geographical boundaries. This was what happened to my girlfriend, Mac Yin Leng. She had an unusual surname and was called Mac by all her friends. Our first teaching posting was to Kelantan. Mac and I took the night express to Kota Baru and arrived early in the morning. As Mac stepped out of the bus at the Kota Baru bus terminal, she was surrounded by quite a number of taxi and *beca* (trishaw) drivers who called her Mac, Mac, Mac. *"Mac, beca?"* *"Mac, mau teksi?"* I shall always remember the look of incredulous surprise on her face and her remark, "Wow, I never realised our Ministry of Education is so efficient! They must have informed them that I'm coming here—look! They all know my name!!"

I thought so too. It took us a while before we found out that in Kelantan, young ladies are all called 'Mek'!

16. SHEDDING THE COLOUR STEREOTYPE

TWENTY years ago, whenever I got into a cab, because of my *kopi susu* (coffee with milk) colouring, I used to be mistaken for a Malay. *"Pergi mana?* (Where do you want to go?)" the taxi man would ask me. Sometimes, I'd answer in Malay, and carry out the whole conversation in Malay, with the driver never guessing that I was actually of Chinese descent.

Sometimes, I'd answer in Cantonese. Then would come the inevitable surprised reply: "Hah? Oh, I thought you were Malay" or comments such as: "Your skin colour is Malay, but your features look Chinese. What are you?"

Twenty years ago, when it came to appearance, there was still a tendency to stereotype a person racially. Malays were supposed to be dusky in complexion, Indians dark-skinned, and Chinese fair. Today, I'm glad to say this type of racial stereotyping does not exist anymore.

These days, it's not such a pat thing trying to tell one's race just by the colour of one's skin. Our colours and shades have swirled and blended in one big melting-pot, and it is quite common to come across fair-skinned Malays and Indians, and Chinese who are tan.

With more and more intermarriages, the features and hues are distinctly getting blurred and it isn't easy to tell exactly what one's race is anymore, not that it matters. In fact, it isn't such a clear-cut matter nowadays when one is asked what one's race is.

When I ask my students to tell the class a little about themselves at the start of a new semester, it is not uncommon to have students who cannot quite pinpoint what race they are: "Well, my mother is Thai-Chinese and my father is half-Scottish. So, what does that make me?"

or "My father is of Malay-English parentage and my mother is a Portuguese Eurasian" or "My grandmother is Kadazan-Chinese, my grandfather has Irish blood and my mother is a Kelantanese Malay. So I really am not quite sure what race I am. I'm a Malaysian."

My reply is usually, "Hurrah for that."

I say hurrah not because the products of these mixed marriages are usually so dropdead good-looking but because it is time we broke away from our traditional mind-sets of thinking of ourselves in terms of race, and start to think of ourselves as one Malaysian race.

By all means, we should be proud of whatever race we come from and always strive to preserve our own racial identity and heritage, but we should also be conscious of the larger scheme of things—that of being a Malaysian.

We feel it often times—this bond that cuts across our racial bloodlines, binding us together—at times of elation and national ecstasy such as when we won back the Thomas Cup in 1992, or in moments of great anguish and despair, for example, during national disasters.

We feel it all the time—this oneness, this Malaysian "sameness" as we go about our day-to-day living, as we sit down and partake of the incredible array of Malaysian foods, as we speak our own special brand of Malaysian English, as we celebrate our festivals and friendships, as we grow up together through trials and tribulations.

I was watching a live band performance at a hotel lounge the other day. The band, a local group, had three lovely female singers—a Chinese, a Malay and an Indian. The band played all types of music, fusing the different ethnic sounds and rhythms together. The Chinese girl sang a Hindustani song, the Malay girl a Mandarin song, the Indian girl a Malay song. Then they all danced the Bhangra. I thought to myself how refreshing that things are not so racially polarised anymore.

Today, when I step into a taxi, still wearing the same shade of *kopi susu* that I was born with, it is now both the driver's and my task to try and figure out what the other is, in order to communicate. Last Saturday, I stepped into a taxi, and thinking that the driver was Chinese, gave my directions in Cantonese. He shook his head, not comprehending what I said. I switched to Malay. Again, he shook his head. Fi-

nally, I spoke in English. He seemed to understand. Aha! I thought—
at long last, 'twas my turn to ask the question which used to be tossed
at me many years ago.

I asked the taxi driver: "Your colouring is like a Chinese but your
features look Malay. What are you?"

He replied: "I am from Myanmar, married to a Northern Malay.
But I'm a Malaysian."

17. OF THATCHED COTTAGES AND BLUEBELLS

IT was a strange sensation—the first time I set foot on England—it felt a little like 'coming home'. There was Big Ben, and Buckingham Palace, and Westminster Abbey, and the Tower of London. There were the turrets and steeples of ancient cathedrals, the red double-decker buses, the taxis and the elegant houses of London. Out in the country, this feeling was even stronger when I first laid eyes on thatched cottages, tumbling rose gardens, stone walls, narrow cobbled roads, quaint hamlets and lavender fields. Why was there this tingle of excitement when I caught my first glimpse of a 'host' of golden daffodils ... waving and dancing in the breeze? Strawberry fields, black-and-white cows grazing on green meadows, crumbling castles, grand country houses, bluebells ... they all seemed so very familiar. Out in Brontë country, amidst brooding heather-draped hills and wild, desolate scenery, why did I feel as if I were at a place revisited?

I remember stopping at a little town called Bakewell in the Peak District to try the famous Bakewell tarts. The lady at the counter looked at me for a moment, then said, "You speak such good English, luv. Where did you learn it from?" I felt a little surprised at the sheer juxtaposition of how much I knew of her country, its culture and traditions ... even felt a part of her country and how little she knew of mine and indeed the historical reason I was speaking English. I told her simply that I came from a school where the medium of instruction was in English, that my parents, teachers and friends were English-speaking, and that the English ruled my country once upon a time. She looked astonished.

We are the products of our upbringing, education and culture, as well as that particular historical milieu that we are born into. What we read and are exposed to seeps into our hearts and minds. Many of us born in the pre-independence and early independence years received an education, conducted in the English medium that was excellent in scope and quality. Textbooks then were written mainly by English authors and it was inevitable that the orientation tended to lean towards England and things English. Even the storybooks, literature and other reading materials were very English in nature and origin. The 'new' literatures of the developing countries and the Commonwealth countries were then at the emergent stage and the literatures of other nations were not so easily available then. Thus, those of my generation were quite familiar with gypsies, caravans, circuses, English 'bobbies', life at English boarding schools—perhaps the influence of authors like Enid Blyton in an era when there were few distractions like the TV or the VCR and reading was the only means of entertainment and escape.

We were more familiar with the animals of the English woodlands—the badger, the dormouse, the rabbit, the hedgehog, the deer—than we were with our own fauna. We knew much of English folklore ... of elfs, goblins, gnomes, fairies, witches and mermaids. We read of swashbuckling knights in shining armour, fair damsels in distress, monarchs, dukes and duchesses, smugglers and one-legged pirates. We were thrilled by the adventures of Robin Hood and his band of merry men and of King Arthur and the Knights of the Round Table. And at the more advanced level, we studied the works of William Shakespeare, were enthralled by the wit of Byron, Oscar Wilde and Shaw, and inspired by the poetry of Wordsworth, Shelley and Keats.

My life has been but enriched, and I do not for a moment negate it in any way. Knowing another culture intimately is an enriching experience and one can only benefit if one opens one's mind. But it does not necessarily nor automatically bring along with it the privilege of belonging to or identifying with that culture. Sometimes, it is like looking through the window into a beautifully decorated home ... you know the details well, are conversant on many of the items in it ... yet you'll never quite belong in that house, simply because you were not born in it in the first place.

Today, I would still recommend the authors, poets, dramatists and writers which I enjoyed. However, today, there is a difference. There are many more choices—prose, verses and views from all parts of the world. It is important that we open the minds of those that we are responsible for to the vast variety of writings and not just stick only to those we were familiar with. All the more so as we live in a multi-cultural society, that we should try and promote a greater consciousness of the complexity and immense diversity of the world we live in and the voices that yearn or clamour to be heard. There are universal truths running through all literature but the perspectives differ, and it is these different cultural perspectives and orientations that are interesting and that will help enlighten us, that we, the human race, are so similar in our own different ways.

18. FEASTING FIASCOS

AT a Chinese wedding dinner, a group of expatriate colleagues of the bridegroom were in a jovial mood. As the bridal couple approached their table in the traditional 'doing the rounds', the expatriates, mostly Westerners, picked up their chopsticks and started banging their plates and glasses, creating quite a din, demanding that the bridegroom kiss the bride. They expected the rest of the guests to join them but to their surprise and much to their discomfort, they only received stares and even some glares from people around them.

To the Chinese, making noise at the dinner table by banging the crockery is a no-no. You can holler *yam seng* (bottoms up) at the top of your lungs or eat and drink as much as you like. Even getting a little drunk is all right but you never, ever beat the crockery with the cutlery (or in this case, the chopsticks). To the Chinese, such an action symbolises bad luck. It bears connotations of hunger and poverty.

Such a cross-cultural mix-up is not uncommon, especially in a country like Malaysia with its rich tapestry of ethnic groups. Another example of a cross-cultural gaffe occurred at yet another Chinese wedding dinner. Things were going along fine until the Master of Ceremonies, who was a good friend of the groom, delivered his speech. It started off well enough. He was eloquent and witty. Then, he started to poke fun at the bridal couple, hinting at their premarital cohabitation lifestyle.

The Master of Ceremonies was of mixed parentage and seemed quite unaware of the culture of Chinese weddings where it is usually the tradition to highlight the virtues and achievements of the bride and groom. Still, the younger members in the audience enjoyed the mild roasting until he started cracking bawdy jokes! The fathers of the bride and groom turned livid shades of purple. Finally, the frantic winks and glares from the bride and groom caused him to stop.

Looking a little puzzled for he was quite sure he had been an entertaining speaker, he went back to his seat.

I was involved in a cross-cultural mix-up once. My friends and I, doing a teaching stint in rural Kelantan, once received an invitation to a *kenduri* (feast). All three of us were Chinese and city slickers, having lived in Kuala Lumpur all our lives. We felt rather fortunate to be able to get a glimpse into the life of the *kampung* and experience a celebration, Malay style.

We told ourselves to be mindful of our manners as the kampung folk were generally more conservative. So, when we sat down to the meal, we made sure that we followed the custom properly. We sat properly, with both our feet pointing in the same direction and not cross-legged as the men. And we made sure we didn't drink the glass of water placed daintily beside a finger bowl in front of each guest.

We had, after all, heard of the infamous story of the Peace Corp lecturer who drank up the glass of water which was meant for washing one's hands. There was a slice of lemon floating in it and he had thought it was lemonade! His Malay host, being gracious, reached out for his own glass of "washing-hands" water and gulped down every drop to save his guest from embarrassment!

My friends and I were treated as special guests and we sat with the hostess who was rather busy supervising things. We ate with our fingers. In the centre of our little circle were placed five dishes. The chicken curry looked extremely delicious but there were only two big pieces of meat in it. Feeling that it would be rude to start dividing the chicken with our bare fingers into three or four parts, I told my friends to go ahead and help themselves, and that I would forego the chicken.

When the hostess came bustling back to our group, she was astonished to see that the plate was empty. She ran back to the kitchen for more chicken and came out with two more pieces of chicken. This time, I helped myself to a piece. Our hostess who had gone off somewhere came back and was shocked to see that another huge piece of chicken had vanished yet again, and rushed off in the direction of the kitchen again.

By then, we began to feel a little worried. How was it that we seemed to be the only group who kept getting our dish replenished? A furtive look around and we almost died of embarrassment. Everyone else had just pinched a little meat off the chicken pieces and placed that portion on one's plate, instead of taking the whole big piece! Thus, we learnt the gentle art of *cubit-cubit* (pinching small pieces of meat from the chicken) fast, and with time, became quite adept at it.

OBSERVATIONS

19. JUST THE RIGHT AMBIENCE

CALL me a stickler for ambience if you wish but wouldn't you agree that somehow, some things just have to be done in the right setting and the right context? Particularly food. Nowadays, it's possible to buy durians, pre-opened and prewrapped with Cling Wrap plastic paper on a styrofoam plate but somehow, it just doesn't taste the same.

When God designed the durian, he definitely had in mind the spirit of friendship and camaraderie that has to be shared when partaking this remarkable fruit. Ever come across anyone eating the durian all by himself? That would be the epitome of loneliness. The durian is a fruit that begs fraternising. It is best eaten with a group of friends or family members, in a casual setting, say, at the durian stall itself, in the open or in the kitchen. Because of its hard thorny covering, it is usually opened on the floor itself with a knife and a wooden stick, surrounded by hungry onlookers, squatting or sitting around, all halfway to Paradise already, just from the incredible and overwhelming smell of the durian.

Opening the durian is such a feat that it begs an audience as well. You've got to find the exact place to make the incision; slit it in the wrong place and it becomes easier to rob a bank. Each wrench, each boring action, each knock plays a crucial part in getting the fruit to open up. When it finally decides to impart its pleasures to the waiting crowd, it does so with the greatest reluctance. A durian does not open up the way, say, a 'duku langsat' does; it opens up slowly, tormentedly, inch by inch, until finally it just gasps wide open.

The durian is also a fruit that demands intense passion about it; you either love it, or you hate it. There is no compromise or fence-sitting when it comes to the durian. Generally, Malaysians of all races love it, while the average *orang puteh* would rather be thrown into the lion's den than spend a night with this fruit.

The sense of expectation when prising the durian open, the *oohs* and *aahs* of delight on seeing the gorgeous yellow fruits nestling in the natural grooves of the durian segments and the tasting of the delicious cloyingly-rich flesh—all these require company. Half the fun is trying out the tastes of each durian and making comments and pronouncements on each fruit, for every durian has its own distinctive taste. If one were to eat durians alone, one would be quite satiated on just one fruit, as well as have no one to make comments to on the quality, texture and taste of the fruit.

Likewise, ever tried eating seafood in an elegant, air-conditioned restaurant with soft music, dim lighting, beautiful table settings and peachy-pink tablecloths? Just doesn't feel quite right, does it? Somehow, one is loathe to dirty the tablecloth or use one's fingers. The best way to dine on seafood, seafood connoisseurs will tell you, is in the open where you can tear at the limbs of the crab like a famished barbarian, gnaw and suck the flesh out of its legs, smash its pincers open with the mallet or hammer or anything heavy that you can lay your hands on, in order to coax out the last shreds of crabmeat still lurking in the corners of the carapace, lick the sweet sour sauce off your fingers, and yet, not feel that you're behaving like some uncouth country bumpkin. When all the crab pieces are gone, and there's that delicious tantalising sauce left, it's quite all right to holler for toast bread and dunk them unceremoniously into that fabulous sauce.

You can also watch the mound of discarded prawn, crab and cockle shells piling up in front of you, without feeling any consternation. The waitress comes along and just bundles up everything in the tablecloth when you leave.

Another Malaysian food that tastes its best in the right setting is the Indian Rojak. There is nothing quite like eating Indian Rojak just after the Rojak man has made it, right there beside the stall itself, usually along the roadside in the shade of a tree. One just stands there or sits by the drain and slurps up the Rojak. And where the Rojak man is, the Indian Chendol man can also be found. Nothing complements the Rojak as superbly as the Indian Chendol. What a heavenly way to take one's lunch, downing the Rojak to the sound of the ice being scraped for the Chendol, enjoying the open air and the unspoken friendship and 'bonding' with the others doing the very same thing.

Therefore, for certain things, one really does not require a sumptuous five-star setting to enjoy them to the fullest. One just needs the right ambience.

20. AT THE PERANAKAN DINING TABLE

AFTER a meal at an Indian banana leaf rice restaurant, how should one fold the banana leaf: should it be away from or towards oneself? Is it impolite to burp during a meal at a Malaysian home?

One area which I find fascinating is the verbal and non-verbal behaviour of Malaysians in an area that is close to their hearts—eating. Each ethnic group has its own etiquette and customs to observe when dining together. I shall discuss only one ethnic group, the Peranakan, or the Babas and Nyonyas, as it is the one that I am most familiar with.

The Peranakan culture is a unique blend of Malay and Chinese cultural elements as a result of inter-marriage between the Chinese and the local women in the days of the Malacca Sultanate five hundred years ago.

When sitting down to a meal in an extended family setting, age takes precedence over gender. Thus, older folks have the honour of taking their seats first followed by the young. It is considered rude if junior members of the family are seated before their elders. In the old days, it was unheard of to have the daughter-in-law already eating when the matriarch of the household had not seated herself yet.

When all are seated, the younger ones are expected to "call" their elders before they tuck into the food. This is again a ritual to show respect for one's elders. It would go something like this, in order of seniority: *Kong, makan* (Grandpa, eat), *Po, makan* (Grandma, eat), *Nya, makan* (Mother, eat), *Toa Chi, makan* (Big Sister, eat), *Ko, makan* (Big Brother, eat), and so on. The elders can respond with a brief reply *makan*, nod slightly or ignore the addressee altogether.

If there are guests present, they should be addressed first. The guests would be suitably impressed that the children of this particular family are well brought up and not *tak senonoh* (unrefined). Like the Malays, the Babas and Nyonyas eat with their fingers. However, the younger generation prefers to use the fork and spoon, which is a practical Malaysian adaptation of the Western way of eating with the fork and knife.

Peranakan food is famous for its delicious piquant taste, combining the best of two cuisines. The Nyonya hostess has to ensure that her guests are well fed. Thus, conversation throughout the meal will be interrupted with the hostess urging her guests to *makan, makan* (eat, eat) or *jangan malu, makan* (don't be shy, eat) or *ambek ini* (take this), followed by her dishing something onto your plate. The hostess keeps watch on her guests diligently, making sure that their needs are catered for. Conversation is not compulsory nor crucial; it the enjoyment of the food that matters.

Having a second helping of rice is a delicate matter if one is a guest. Having seconds is a compliment to the hostess. It implies that the food is so good that you want some more. Traditionally, she would be a disappointed Nyonya if none of her guests take a second helping because she takes great pride in her cooking. She might even ask you point-blank, *"Mengapa? Ta' sedap-ehh?"* (What's the matter? Is it not good?). And whatever your reason, you'll have to say, *"Bukan, dah kenyang"* (No, it's just that I'm full). And despite your protests, the hostess will still attempt to pile some rice on your plate. To indicate to the hostess that you've got enough, you have to use your right hand and gently attempt to 'block' the advancing scoops of rice.

At the end of the meal, one is expected not to leave anything behind on one's plate. Bits of rice left are frowned upon, and *anak dara* (young girls) are admonished and warned that they will end up either pockmarked or married to pockmarked husbands if they don't clear their plates.

Another superstition is that one should not pile empty plates on top of one another on the dining table. The superstitious Nyonya believes that one's debts will pile up like the plates. This is observed only amongst the very traditional, and many of the younger generation are not aware of this belief.

Of course, many of the Peranakan customs and food etiquette are no longer practised today in these more frenetic times. Extended families have become more the exception than the norm, especially in urban areas. In extended families, it is more a case of the mother-in-law serving the daughter-in-law nowadays because most modern young women go to work!

Today, we have another type of food culture with its own set of verbal and non-verbal behaviour, which cuts across all cultures. This is the fast-food culture where to get your food, you have to join a queue. A huge wall menu faces you and you have to decide what to order quickly so as not to interrupt the brisk, mechanical pace of things.

When you reach the counter, to the tune of the cash register and the sounds of cheery plastic voices going "Good evening, Ma'am, can I take your order, Ma'am?" or "Good evening, Sir, can I help you, Sir?" you place your order.

And in just a minute or two, you walk away with your meal wrapped in paper or stored in styrofoam boxes, and are told by those same voices to have a nice day although whether your day turns out to be nice or not, no one gives a hoot. The strangest thing about it all is— don't our kids just love it?!

21. WILL YOU SIGN
MY AUTOGRAPH?

EXCHANGING autographs does not seem to be such a popular activity amongst schoolchildren nowadays. Of course, getting the autographs of celebrities such as movie stars, famous singers and sports personalities is still actively pursued. But what about getting the autographs of one's friends, teachers, and other persons who are not necessarily famous but precious to you?

Exchanging autographs is an activity which ought to be encouraged. It requires the child to be constructive and to create something which will be put on permanent record in the autograph book. It also touches the child in the affective domain as it requires the child to think about his feelings for the friend whose autograph he is signing, what he wants to express, and how to go about saying it in words.

The collecting of autographs should not just be confined to famous personalities. It is the autographs of friends and loved ones that are the most cherished in the end.

I was browsing through an old autograph book of mine from primary school days a weekend ago, and it brought back sweet memories of my friends and teachers. Below is a collection of some of the well-known autograph verses which were quite popular in the 1960s. It is not known how they originated or who composed these stanzas, but they were passed on from one person to another through the autograph books and have therefore become 'classics':

On Friendship:

True friends are like diamonds
Precious and rare

False friends are like autumn leaves
Scattered everywhere.

Far out in the ocean
There lies a rock
On it is written
Forget me not.

Make new friends
Keep the old
One is silver
The other is gold.

On Remembrance:

When the golden sun is setting
And your mind from troubles free
When you're sometimes thinking of others
Will you sometimes think of me?

I write not for beauty
I write not for fame
But for Remembrance
I just sign my name.

Far away in a forgotten land
You see the writing of my hand
Though my face you cannot see
Dearest ..., remember ME!

The Ones with Humour:

Drink hot coffee
Drink hot tea
Burn your lips
And remember me.

Policeman, policeman
Do your duty
Here comes ...
The Malaysian Beauty!

Fall from a tree
Fall from above
Fall from anywhere
But don't fall in love.

Many a ship was lost at sea
Through loss of sail or rudder
Many a boy has lost a girl
Through winking at another!

An autograph which I find particularly beautiful is a verse written in my father's autograph book. It was written on the 26th of July 1941 by a childhood friend of my father's, and the words of his autograph entry still ring true to this day. It is on how precious and yet fragile true friendship is, and it goes like this:

Break not the friendship of a friend in vain
The same friendship you will never regain,
For true friendship once broken like a china bowl,
Can never never again be made whole.
It can be mended like the china bowl, it's true
But the parts mended will always remain in view.

I owned my first autograph book when I was eleven years old. It was a birthday present from my parents. The first persons I asked to sign my autograph were my parents. My mother composed a lovely little verse for me which I share here with you:

To my dear little girl on her eleventh birthday,

Have a smile for everyone
Be he big or small
Like the rays of the sun
Which shine not for one
But shine for all.

Lots of love,
Mama

Then I approached my father. He thought for awhile then penned something and returned the book to me. I eagerly turned to the page where he'd written, expecting a verse or some flowery prose. I was stunned when I saw his entry—it was stark, comprising only six words:

Gold is where you find it.

Papa

I was disappointed ... why had he written so little? Besides, being only eleven then, I didn't understand what it meant. I took it at its literal level. " You mean I can really find gold? How can that be, Papa? I don't understand ... "

He looked at me and said softly, with the wisdom of a man who has lived and loved and found his happiness in his wife and children, "Someday you'll know what I mean, Kim."

Today, my parents are no more. While I have so many wonderful memories of them, the writings of their hand are few. Those two pages with those two special messages are deeply treasured—one, a message of spreading joy and cheer and the other, which I had found so difficult to understand then, hits me on the head now in its shining truth and simplicity.

22. THE CHANGING SEASONS

I N a temperate country, you can tell the changing of the seasons from Mother Nature herself. In Spring, tiny budding shoots emerge from the ground, and little green leaves appear on long-slumbering branches. In Autumn, Nature paints the country in shades of gold, russet and brown. Trees shed their leaves and animals of the temperate forests prepare to hibernate during the long, cold winters. In Malaysia, we don't have the four seasons but we have a different kind of seasons and that is seasons based on the various festivals and celebrations of the various races. We have indeed quite a number. With so many, how do we keep track? Well, Nature does not do that job here; the department stores, hotels and shopping complexes do it for us. Not all the seasons though, basically the ones that generate the most spending power.

I had not even gotten over the Lantern Festival season when one day last October, I stepped into a department store and was amazed to find that yet another season had come and gone. All traces of the Lantern Festival which had been hanging around for all to see had been obliterated! All the bright red lanterns, the colourful Japanese paper ones and even the grotesque plastic Ultramans and Batmans had been put away. And the mooncakes—where were the mooncakes? They had all disappeared! I had not quite reached satiety on my favourite double *tan wong* (golden egg yolks) mooncakes yet ... and what were they busy putting up? Christmas decorations!

Christmas already? And it was only October! But, yes, there they were putting up the Christmas trees, twinkling lights, bright baubles, plastic mistletoe and holly, being directed by a slim androgynous supervisor, an 'artsy-tartsy' type in tight jeans, with two earstuds on one ear. The bright red shelves had been replaced by bright red and green shelves and were being filled with cute little teddy bears, trolls, candles, Christmas mugs and plates and woollen stockings. A styrofoam Santa Claus figure with rosy cheeks and twinkling eyes stood in a corner next to baskets of Made-in-Taiwan Christmas trinkets, and salegirls dressed in Santarina costumes and knee-high boots were walking about, promoting their products.

In another shopping complex, why, it was practically snowing! Stepping into the shopping complex from the hot humid weather outside, I saw that the whole atrium had been decorated with cardboard cut-outs of snowflakes and cotton balls. There was snow, snow, snow or should I say, cotton, cotton, cotton everywhere ... draping the shelves, doorways and Christmas trees. Tourists from the cold climes must have been quite amused. On second thoughts, maybe not so amused after having paid a lot of money to escape the sludge and snow only to encounter more 'snow' here, albeit of the cottonwool variety.

At the Bukit Bintang Plaza, I experienced an unusual experience. I was browsing through the book section of a department store. The place was beautifully togged up for Christmas: lined with wallpaper of English country roses and stocked with fine English bone china and piles of potpourri. Big wicker baskets overflowing with dried flowers were placed at strategic corners. As I swung open the door to leave, there just a floor below, was a stage show featuring a group of Indian classical dancers. The show was in celebration of Deepavali, an important festival of the Hindus, which was just two months before Christmas in 1993.

I paused. Standing in the doorway, I savoured the experience, one half of me lingering over the beautiful Christmas ambience created in that store with its soft colours, fragrant smells and the strains of time-less Christmas carols; and the other half of me captivated by the Indian classical dancers, their colourful costumes and intricate steps, the flash of exotic *kohl*-lined eyes, the whirl and swirl of colours, the pulsating pounding of the drums, the earthy rhythm of the music, the sensuality and vibrance of it all.

Hot on the heels of Christmas comes Chinese New Year. Christmas is supposed to last for twelve days, but after about five days or so, the 'store decorators' are hard at work again. Out go the tartans, the dried flowers and Christmas trees. The colour combination of Red and Green goes out, and in comes the colour Red. From a soft, wintery feel, with smells of pine and sounds of silver bells, we are whooshed into Chinoserie in a big way. The transformation is sudden, almost overnight; there is no shedding of gentle autumn leaves nor the melting of cottonwool. Step into a department store or shopping complex just a week after Christmas and the message screams at you that another season has arrived.

Crates of *kums* (mandarin oranges) are stacked high to the ceiling. Big wooden barrels of dried lychees, longans, red and black melon seeds, peanuts and dried mushrooms are displayed conspicuously. All the Chinese New Year delicacies such as abalone, shark fin, sea cucumber, pacific clams, bamboo shoots, waxed ducks and waxed Chinese sausages are now in overflowing abundance. Stacks of cakes and cookies in bright red boxes and carbonated drinks stand ready for the frenzied shopping to begin. The decor is always in red with decorations ranging the whole gamut such as dragons, phoenixes, lions, goldfishes, gold carps, horses, children in Oriental costumes, fans, umbrellas, cherry blossoms or pussy willow. Everywhere, red *ang pows* and paper firecrackers hang from the ceiling. And in the background one can hear the songs associated with the Chinese New Year, and the exciting music of the gongs, flutes, cymbals and drums.

This year, Hari Raya Puasa also comes hot on the heels of Chinese New Year. The store people will have to work very hard again. All the red 'ang pows' will have to be replaced with green ones. All things red will be stored away and in comes the colour Green. The ambience will have to be changed to that of perhaps a grand Malay palace with exotic *kain songket* and gold decorations or a Malay *kampung* atmosphere with decorations of *ketupat*, batik and *bungga mangga*. The cakes and cookies of Hari Raya take pride of place. From the Rum-pum-pum-pums and Tra-la-la-la-las of December to the *gong xi, gong xi, gong xi nis* of February, the music for March will soon be the catchy *Selamat*

Hari Raya by Saloma, the warm caressing tones of P. Ramlee, and the beautiful songs of Sudirman.

And all who step in will know that yet another season has gone by and another season has arrived.

23. 'ANG POW' POW WOW

THERE are some things about Chinese New Year that a child particularly enjoys. New clothes, great food, no school, and no scolding nor nagging from Mum or Dad as it's considered inauspicious to start the Lunar New Year in a grumpy, grouchy mood. Then, there are the *ang pows* from the adults. *Ang pows* are little red packets containing money, given out to children as a token of generosity and prosperity.

One great perk in staying single is that you get to receive *ang pows* during Chinese New Year! No matter how old you are or how fat your pay-check is, to the Chinese, as long as you're not married, you are considered a 'child' in the eyes of society and therefore you deserve an *ang pow!* However, it is not without a lot of haranguing, teasing and nagging from your Aunties even as they dish out the *ang pows* to you.

"*Heiyah, when is your turn to give ang pow-ah? Faster get married-lah! Don't be so choosy!*"

Or "*Aai-yo, terrible-lah you. Every year I have to give you ang pow. I rugi-lah like this.*"

Or "*Quickly-ah, Quickly-ah. Make sure you get married this year, ah. Your Uncle and I still waiting for your red invitation card.*"

It is of course all done good-naturedly, and you are supposed to receive the *ang pow* in an equally benign spirit. Should you be embarassed about it , or wish to feign embarassment, you could always demur, "*No need-lah, Auntie, I'm so big already. Shy only ...*", and you'll be instantly scolded and told that you must "*take, take. How can don't take? You're still considered a child, you know*", and you'll find the *ang pow* pressed into your palm or slipped into your pocket. Well, why argue when you're being showered with money?

Of course, the moment you get married, and Chinese New Year comes around, you are considered an adult overnight and you'll then have to distribute *ang pows* just like everyone else. One compensation would be that now, you could also start nagging all those cousins of yours who are still dragging their feet regarding matrimony.

The giving out of *ang pows* to children is a pleasurable experience. However, if you come across kids of the really mercenary kind, then you wish you could snatch back the *ang pow* from their greedy hands. A kid is supposed to receive an *ang pow*, thank the giver, then put away his *ang pow* immediately. No matter how curious he is about its contents, it is considered unbecoming to show interest in it. There are some little horrors, though, who think nothing of holding it up to the light, as soon as they have received the *ang pow*, trying to figure out how much is contained inside. Some even tear open the *ang pows* to take a direct look! And if the *ang pow* is heavy (kids are smart nowadays), they know that the heavier the *ang pow* the less it contains. This is because the one-ringgit denomination comes only in coin form and so, a two-ringgit *ang pow* would certainly be heavier than say, a five- or ten-ringgit *ang pow* today. The smart aleck, on receiving the *ang pow* might say, *"Cheh, only two dollars!"* making it quite stressful for the poor *ang pow*-giving adults.

Kids should realise that the giving of *ang pows* is a graceful tradition, and not a money-making operation. But then, who knows? From such audacious beginnings might be born our future generation of intrepid entrepreneurs, corporate leaders and investment bankers!

One aspect of Chinese New Year which I enjoyed very much as a child (and which, I confess, I still do today) are the lion dances staged by various lion dance troupes and associations throughout the fifteen days of Chinese New Year. Just the sound of the drums would send my pulse racing. How I love the clash of the gongs, the cymbals and the pounding of those huge drums that have to be pushed around on wheels. It is a beautiful art form, the way the two dancers have to dance in perfect synchronisation, two bodies moving and prancing as if of one body and one mind, in time to the pounding rhythm of the 'music'. The way the lion prances and frolics about, flutters its eyelashes, blinks its eyes, wiggles its ears and preens itself—it's easy for the spectators to get swept away by the theatricality of it all, forgetting that there are two persons, working very hard underneath the robe.

The music rises to a crescendo, climaxing when the lion finally gets the lettuce and the *ang pow* which are usually tied to a pole, requiring some acrobatics before the lion can grab the *ang pow*. Then, when the lion is 'chewing' away at the lettuce, lying flat on its tummy, its eyelashes fluttering with delight over its find (the performer carrying the lion head has to shred the lettuce with his hands and occasionally throw out some bits and pieces), the music softens, and the cymbals and drums are hushed. When the lion is 'full', it leaps up to its feet again, prances about and does some spectacular leaps, rising to its full height, then does a few bows as if expressing its gratitude to the owner of the home or shop, before it moves on to another destination.

It is not uncommon to come across lion dance troupes that are multiracial in composition these days. A discernible trend is that many of the various art forms of our country are being shared and enjoyed by all, regardless of race, and this should be encouraged for a truly Malaysian identity.

While there are many excellent lion dance troupes in existence today, I've also come across some that are amateurish and unprofessional. Some put on a very poor show, grab the *ang pow*, then quickly move on without bothering to go through the movements required.

Once, I was stunned and walked away, aghast, because so inexperienced were the performers that the whole show was poorly executed and the main performer actually fell off the knees of his partner, when trying to reach the *ang pow* and the pole was only at ground level! Another instance, the crowd that had gathered was disappointed for the main performer 'took off' his lion head, climbed up the pole where the *ang pow* was strung, then had his friends pass the lion head up to him and he put it back on, not realising that the illusion of the dancing, prancing big pussycat was totally ruined. I'm no expert on lion dances but I feel it's important that certain standards should be maintained to preserve the dignity and magic of this enthralling art form.

The artistry of the dance, not the *ang pow*, should be the overriding factor.

24. BELOVED BUSYBODIES

W HEN the end of the year is around the corner, it means that soon it will be time for family reunions again. For those of the fairer sex, who are single and available, or single but not necessarily available, it's that time of the year again when your marital status, or rather the lack of it, comes under scrutiny. Come Christmas, New Year, Chinese New Year or Hari Raya, families and clans get together and then the finely-tuned torture begins!

Aunties and grandaunts will look askance at a particular part of your anatomy, specifically the fourth finger of your left hand, hoping to see an engagement ring. If there is no such adornment, they will tut-tut-tut and query you point-blank, "So, when are you getting married-ah?" If you are fairly attractive and fairly shapely, they will assume that you are drowning in beaux, and advise you to snap the biggest fish available, as if the decision were as simple as deciding between the *bawal puteh* or the *ikan kembong* at the wet market. "Aiiyah ... don't be so choosy-*lah*," they'll urge as if you were having the greatest time 'eeny-meeny-minor-mo'-ing your boyfriends.

"Hai-yah ... I tell you what-*lah* ... marry the tycoon's son-*lah*, the one with the buck teeth! What more you want?" advises your well-meaning aunt triumphantly.

"But I don't love him!" you protest.

"Love! Love! That's the trouble with you young people nowadays. No need for love one-*lah* ... take it from me. You tink your Uncle and I got love ah when we got married. We only met on the wedding day! Now you see ... we are married for so ... oo long already. You young people talk love, love, get married and then, next day divorce!"

If you are unfairly unattractive, then the urgings become even more frantic. "Any fish will do, just grab it" seems to be the message.

"Aiiyah ... don't be so fussy-*lah*, you're not getting any younger you know," they'll cajole and coax as if landing a husband were as easy as going to the market to buy a fish, any fish!

Finally, for reasons of love or otherwise, one day, you do decide to tie the nuptial knot. Your relatives will give you some time ... nine months to a year or two, and then the queries start again. This time, they will look at another part of your anatomy—your stomach. If it's still reasonably flat, they'll ask you, "So, when's your first one-ah?"

"I've already got my first one," you reply, you think, wittily.

"Hah?? No ... I don't mean husband-*lah*. Aiyo!! You-ah! I mean ... when are you going to start a family?"

If you tell them you really can't bear children, well, that would depend on what kind of 'bearing' you're talking about! If you mean you can't bear the thought of having those screechy brats around your neck and feet, and don't plan to have any children ever, they will look at you horrified as if you were something unnatural and then promptly worry about who will inherit your property. If you tell them you intend to give it all away to charity, they will look at you as if you were the most uncharitable person around not to want to give it to your children, whom, in the first place you weren't planning to have.

If it was the other type of 'bearing' and you tell them that you adore children but that making babies was harder than you thought, you will get all sorts of advice ranging from consuming *kacang kuda* to ginseng to royal jelly. Be assured that all the tips on 'productivity' will focus on food. Mention sex, and they'll look at you as if it were some strange alien food, quite unheard of, and totally irrelevant. You ask nonchalantly, "And so, Auntie, you have eleven children. What position would you recommend? ... Auntie ... er ... auntie, hey, where did she run off to?!!"

If or when you're finally pregnant, your whole appearance will be commented upon and discussed scientifically. If you look tidy and radiant and your tummy is neat and round, chances are you've got a boy! If you look all blotchy and spotty and ugly, and your tummy's all over the place, then it's a girl. (Even symptoms can be sexist!)

After the birth of the first child, phew, peace at last. That's what you think. Well, give yourself a year or two, and then come the 'acu-puncturing' questions again—gentle, harmless but pressure-exerting.

"So, when's your next one?"

Aaaargggh!

If you've got one, you really ought to have another—one's too lonesome. If you've got two girls—Aiyo! *Rugi besar*, girls get married out, you know!" or "What about the family name?!"—you've got to try for a boy! If you've got two boys, well, 'sons are sons till they get them-selves wives, daughters are daughters all their lives', so you've got to get a girl.

Well, isn't life just great? Better to have bodies, no matter how 'busybody', to fuss and worry and cluck over you than to have nobody at all. And no matter how much you swear you'll never ask anyone those questions that you've been subjected to, one day, when your hair is flecked with silver and your memory dims a little, you too might want to prod along the next generation and ask, "So, when are you get-ting married-ah?"

25. NO MORE HANG-UPS OVER OUR COLONIAL PAST

W E'VE outgrown it, expunged it. Like a case of bad indigestion, we've finally gotten it out of our system. By 'it', I mean the hang-up we have about our colonial past. Once, we wanted to obliterate all trace or memory of it. We wanted to eradicate whatever we could that reminded us that the British colonial masters once ruled this land.

Changing the names of roads named after certain *orang putih* was one way. Many roads, particularly in Kuala Lumpur, that bore the names of personalities from the colonial era, were renamed after local personae and historical figures. Thus, Jalan Mountbatten, named after Lord Louis Mountbatten, was renamed Jalan Tun Perak; Treacher road, named after William Hood Treacher, a British resident of Selangor, became Jalan Sultan Ismail; Jalan Weld, named after Sir Frederick Weld, was renamed Jalan Raja Chulan; and Shaw Road, named after Bennett Eyre Shaw, the first headmaster of the Victoria Institution, was renamed Jalan Hang Tuah, after our Malay folk hero.

Perhaps the most famous (or perhaps infamous, depending on whose side you are on) *coup d'etat* was the renaming of Jalan Birch. This road was originally named after James Birch, a British resident of Perak who was assassinated by Maharajalela when Birch was taking his bath (that is what the history books written by the British say). After the British Empire in this part of the world faded into the sunset, the tables were turned—villain (according to the British) became hero (according to us), and hero turned villain instead! What was formerly Jalan Birch was renamed Jalan Maharajalela.

Today, we really don't get too uncomfortable or hot under the collar if we encounter reminders of a distant time in our history. This is perhaps a sign of our new-found confidence, a feeling of our own strength and security. We are, after all, the shapers of our own destiny, no matter what the past was. Everywhere, there are signs that we have made peace with ourselves, and with our past.

Today, grand old hotels and restaurants that were the gathering places of the cream of society during the colonial era are being restored to their former glory and splendour. The old Coliseum Hotel and Restaurant along Jalan Tuanku Abdul Rahman is a popular destination if you want to take a peek into the place where once the cream of British society wined and dined. The elegant E&O Hotel in Penang is another venue for the traveller who seeks the old world ambience. At the Carcosa, the former home of the British High Commissioner and now a grand hotel for the rich and famous, the present-day elite gather to enjoy their Earl Greys and nibble on dainty scones and muffins for that very English ritual called 'tea' or for 'curry tiffin' on Sunday afternoons.

Clubbing, an essentially British tradition, is quite the norm nowadays with the affluent middle class, and retreating to the hill stations such as the Cameron Highlands, Fraser's Hill or Penang Hill for a brief sojourn from the oppressive lowlands, once a practice of the white man, is a popular pastime with the locals too. A fondness for things British is also reflected in the architectural designs of houses and apartments today that strive for the Tudor or Georgian or the English Country House look.

Recently, a half-page newspaper advertisement for a particular brand of apparel caught my attention. The name of the brand was British India. The advertisement showed an old black-and-white portrait of British imperialdom, posing stiffly with their spouses dressed in their fines with hats and plumes and long white gloves, as well as an assortment of Indian royalty at that time—a number of turbanned and bejewelled sultans, maharajahs and nabobs.

The words on the advert read: "Presenting British India. An Era of Racism, Oppression, Injustice and Nice Outfits." One can't help but smile at the tongue-in-cheek tone of the ad. Well, yes, we are indeed getting it out of our system. We are even cracking jokes at its expense!

26. HAVING TOO MUCH OF A GOOD THING

PERHAPS it was a reaction to a childhood deprivation of mine. When I was a child, there was never quite enough of sparklers to go around whenever we celebrated Chinese New Year. So, last Chinese New Year, I decided to buy a bundle of sparklers for my son, so that he could play to his heart's content. I bought about ten packets of sparklers. As there were ten in each packet, that meant a hundred to play with!

We started off happily. I lit the sparklers for him and we had great fun twirling the sparklers, making neon patterns in the night. By the time we reached the fifth packet, my son was getting quite satiated and by the ninth packet and the ninetieth sparkler, both of us were absolutely fed-up with sparklers—which led me to realise that too much of a good thing can be bad.

I learnt this valuable lesson too from my Chestnut Experience. I absolutely love roasted chestnuts. It could be because it seemed like I never had enough of it when I was a child. I remember many years ago during the chestnut season, my father would sometimes walk out to the Pavilion Cinema where there was a hawker stall selling the most fabulous roasted chestnuts.

They were fragrant in a smoky sort of way, juicy and tender. Three of us kids would wait eagerly for his return. When father got back, he'd distribute the precious chestnuts to the older folk first. As we were an extended family, there were many mouths to feed—Grandpa, Grandma, Mother (who'd usually "pass" seeing the children's expectant faces) and my *amah*.

Then came our turn—my sister, brother and I, jumping and squirming with excitement. Papa was great at making everything a game with us. He wasn't a gambler but he certainly had a gambler's streak in him. He loved bringing in the element of chance, the luck of the draw in whatever he did.

He'd divide the chestnuts into three piles—one with the most chestnuts, then one somewhere midway, and then the pile with the least. Of course, we would all eye the biggest pile hungrily. There was no favouritism. We had to compete for the fist prize.

This we had to do by playing the *La-la-li-la-tum pong* game. The one who lost first was awarded the smallest pile, much to his or her dismay. Then the remaining two had to go into the final round—by playing the *One Two Som* game. It was terribly exciting going *One Two Som, One Two Som* as Bird, Stone and Water fought it out, as indicated by the shape of our hands. Of course. the winner got the biggest pile of chestnuts!

As we tucked happily into the chestnuts, sometimes Papa would trick us by yelling, "Look, look! There's a pink elephant up in the sky!" Three gullible souls would look out the window and Papa would swipe some of our chestnuts from our individual piles!

So, with all that competition, little wonder then that I developed a passion for those delicious, finger-scorching hot chestnuts.

Not too long ago, on one of my occasional forays into the *pasar malam* (night market), a waft of that familiar roasty chestnut-ty smell filled the air. I sniffed my way to a hawker busily roasting chestnuts, swirling them in a blackened wok. I decided to give myself a treat and bought a kilo of it.

That night, with no one particularly interested in the chestnuts except myself, I sat there at the kitchen table and stuffed myself silly with chestnuts.

But the magic wasn't there.

There was no scarcity, only abundance; there was no finiteness, only a huge infinite-looking pile of nuts staring at me, demanding to be eaten. Somehow, they just didn't taste as delicious as they used to many years ago.

And so the lesson I've learnt is a simple one. If I want my child to appreciate a certain thing, giving him more of it may not necessarily be better. In fact, one might even rob the child of that special joy—the joy of getting something that one yearns for but which doesn't come too easily.

This year, I did not overindulge. My son received only three packets of sparklers to play with. As for his mother, no more kilogrammes of chestnuts ... well, perhaps half a kati the next time around.

27. THAT MAGNIFICENT SCHOOL SPIRIT

IN 1993, I had the rare privilege of attending the centenary dinners of two great schools—the Bukit Bintang Girls' School and the Victoria Institution. On both occasions, I was struck by that intangible quality that seems to be on its way to extinction nowadays—the school spirit. When the school anthem at each centenary dinner was played, men and women rose to their feet and stood at attention, their faces shining with pride. As they sang the school song of their *alma mater*, they were transported back to those precious school days, a time so distant in their lives and yet so poignantly meaningful.

At the centenary dinner of the Bukit Bintang Girls' School, my *alma mater*, when the familiar strains of the school anthem filled the air, the sense of joy and pride was indescribable. It seemed as if our hearts would burst as our voices soared in unison ... little bits of words haltingly remembered at first, then gaining in strength and volume as the memories came surging back. Many had tears in their eyes, overwhelmed by their emotions ...

> BBGS we pledge to thee
> Our love and toil in the years to be,
> When we are grown and take our place
> As loyal women with our race.
>
> Father in Heaven, who lovest all,
> Oh, help thy children when they call,
> That they may build from age to age
> An undefiled heritage.
>
> Teach us to bear the yoke in youth
> With steadfastness and careful truth

That in our time, thy grace may give
The truth whereby the nations live.

Teach us delight in simple things
And mirth that has no bitter springs
Forgiveness free of evil done
And love to all men 'neath the sun.

As schoolgirls, we sang the school anthem every Monday at assembly, making sure we shaped our words properly with our mouths, under the eagle eye of our headmistress who would pace the stage, looking out for anyone who did not know the school song. Now that we the 'old girls' have indeed grown, and taken our place as fellow Malaysians, the words hold an even deeper meaning.

The hall of the Putra World Trade Centre was filled to capacity that night. Many more who had wanted to attend had to be turned away. When I stepped into the hall that night, it was like a step through a journey of twenty years, back to those schoolgirl days. Here were all the familiar faces ... headmistresses, teachers, schoolfriends, prefects, librarians, school athletes and school personalities. Friends whom I had not met for years appeared before my eyes. Many ex-BBGS girls had travelled vast distances to attend this very special occasion, flying in from countries as far as China, England and the United States.

What was it that brought us back, from all the corners of the globe? What was this special quality that bound all of us—women from all walks of life, from a wide spectrum of occupations such as CEOs, directors, diplomats, doctors, educationists, managers, homemakers, lawyers, scientists, accountants, entrepreneurs, missionaries, artists?

It wasn't just a pledge, it was a deep-rooted, unshakeable feeling of love and loyalty for our school that brought us back together, and a desire to honour and pay tribute to a great institution that had shaped our lives during those crucial formative years.

At the VI centenary dinner, the same feeling of pride in one's *alma mater* was evident. Men turned misty-eyed, singing in one mighty resonance the VI anthem. In the gathering were corporate leaders, politicians, famous surgeons, multi-millionaires, judges, Datuks, Tan Sris and even the richest man in the world, the Sultan of Brunei. It wasn't an ordinary dinner function, it was an extraordinary event, never to take place again until another hundred years.

It must be conceded that some of the finest schools in the country—mission as well as non-mission schools—were established during the colonial era. The traditions and value systems of these schools were passed on from generation to generation. Principals and teachers were highly dedicated to their chosen vocation. Tremendous emphasis was placed on discipline and the pursuit of excellence, and staff usually served for a long time, giving a sense of history and continuity to the school.

Today, one hears of rampant indiscipline in schools, of teachers and principals being transferred about, of relocation of schools and students, and saddest of all, of demoralised teachers biding their time until retirement. The teaching profession has lost much of its allure, attracting only a handful of those who are truly dedicated. With the advent of the age of materialism, students seems to have lost that traditional respect that once held students enthralled of their teachers. Many principals and teachers lack that burning commitment to their profession.

I fear one day, schools will, with some exceptions, become like factories, churning out students by the thousands, but never quite making that special imprint on the heart and mind of the student. Will the school spirit too become a thing of the past?

28. LANGUAGES NOT PASSED ON

I read somewhere that the dialects of the world were fast disappearing. Linguistic experts warned that up to 95 per cent of the world's 6,000 languages will be either extinct or on the road to extinction. According to researchers, between 20 and 50 per cent of the world's languages are no longer being learnt by children. I, for one, must be held guilty for not perpetuating my own vernacular tongues to the next generation.

I grew up in a colourful, polyglot world. Everyday, there were at least three to four languages and dialects being used in my home, and I grew accustomed to the cadences and sounds of the different languages, without any confusion or discomfort.

My father and grandfather were typical Babas from Malacca, and could speak only English and Baba Malay. Mother was a Peranakan Chinese with her roots in Penang, and could speak English, Penang Hokkien, Cantonese and, after her marriage, mastered Baba Malay as well. Grandma spoke English, Hokkien, Cantonese, Baba Malay as well as some Hakka. All of them could speak Malay, as it was quite similar to the Baba patois.

It was interesting how each member of my family had a fixed mind-set about which language to use when speaking to a particular family member. Father spoke only Baba Malay to his parents, but switched to English with Mother. Mother used Baba Malay when talking with her father-in-law, Hokkien with her mother-in-law, and English with her husband.

As for us, the children, the predominant language was English and a smattering of Hokkien with our parents, Baba Malay with Grandpa and, for some strange reason, Cantonese when speaking to Grandma. This was practised because, I think, our elders wanted us to acquire at least some basic Cantonese.

I was educated in the English medium, and learnt Malay as a second language in school. And so I grew up with this array of languages and dialects tucked under my belt. I wasn't particularly exceptional in the vernacular dialects—friends still chuckle whenever I speak Cantonese saying that I speak it with an accent—but managed to get by. Being educated in the English medium though, English soon took over and became the dominant language in my life. I live, love, laugh and weep in English, think in English, and dream in English, with occasional strands of thoughts and concepts in Chinese or Malay. I am nowhere an exception—most people of my generation and many generations before me went through the same process, and operate in much the same manner.

What strikes me as an interesting and rather worrying phenomenon though is that having come from such a multi-lingual background, only one language is spoken, i.e. English, in my home today. My husband and I speak English to each other. We operate in an English-speaking world with friends and relatives all speaking in English. Our child, fours years old, knows only one language, English, and no dialects at all. We tried speaking some Cantonese but felt rather awkward and so did not persist. But I comfort myself that when my child goes to school, he will learn formal Malay and Mandarin. That would be quite a lot of languages for one so young and quite a Malaysian spread.

"What about his mother tongue then? What about his own vernacular dialects?" my foreign friends ask me, "Won't they all be lost?"

An acquaintance from the United States who had just been in Malaysia for a few days looked at me with raised eyebrows when I told her my son spoke only English.

I put myself in her shoes and realise it must have seemed rather odd to her, coming all the way from an English-speaking part of the world to this part of exotic Asia only to find a whole generation of children, the offspring of English-educated parents, communicating in English!

The question then that has to be posed is how much importance one places on one's own vernacular dialect. Is it important enough for you to make a conscious effort to teach and impart it to the next generation? In many cases, the question may not even be that of prioritising, but that of time. In this rat race world where we whiz through life at a breathless pace, just making "quality time" for our children is no mean feat, no matter what language or dialect is used!

My friend, Dr Zain, a Kelantanese Malay, who lives and works in Kuala Lumpur and speaks impeccable English, laments that his children do not know his Kelantanese Malay dialect.

Sheila, a Tamil Indian friend, got a mini "sermon" the other day from the Indian man selling dried goods at the *pasar tani*. He had asked Sheila's five-year-old son something in Tamil in a friendly way, but the little boy had stared at him, not understanding a word of Tamil, and had responded in English.

Why should we care? is a question that we could pose as a counter-argument. Isn't life complex enough without having to worry about all sorts of things? Isn't life tough enough for Malaysian children as they must have a command of Malay, the national language, English, the second language, and for those in the Chinese- and Tamil-medium schools, a third language as well?

Well, according to Dr Michael Krauss, a language researcher at the University of Alaska, the first argument is that the world would be a less interesting place to live in. The second is that mankind's way of thinking in different ways would be significantly reduced and, lastly, he argues that we do not yet realise that we live in an ecosystem of human diversity which is essential for our survival.

I agree with Dr Krauss' first point. Imagine Malaysia, with its incredible diversity of languages gradually losing its multi-dialectical flavour. Imagine stepping into Kelantan and never hearing that fascinating and inimitable Kelantanese Malay dialect. Imagine losing the Terengganu or Kedah Malay dialects. And what about the myriad of languages and dialects of the ethnic groups of East Malaysia?

The Peranakan patois—a delightful mixture of Malay, Hokkien and some English—itself is dying out. The list of dialects spoken in Malaysia is a long one and who knows how many of these dialects will be around by the middle of the next century?

Sometimes, one has to leave one's country before one can truly appreciate one's cultural heritage. An interesting thing happened at my place last December when two of my first cousins, both married to foreigners and residing overseas, came home to Malaysia for a visit. One cousin had married a New Zealander and the other an English girl. They came over to my place one day with their families. It was intriguing, to say the least—the cousin married to the English girl refused to speak in any other language except Cantonese to his two young children while the cousin married to the Kiwi spoke nothing but Hakka to her little girl and boy. So there I was, surrounded by four blond and brunnete blue-eyed and hazel-eyed children with Caucasian features, all jabbering away in strongly-accented Cantonese and Hakka, while my little boy, with his typical Asian looks, was jabbering away in English! Now who was the native English speaker here?

Ah well, there's always tomorrow ... Tomorrow, if I could but find the time, I shall seat my little boy upon my lap and teach him a little of the dialects that his Grandpa and Grandma and great-grandparents taught me.

29. BAD HABITS DIE HARD

Picture this. The year: 2020. The place: Kuala Lumpur. Imagine we are approaching the capital. From afar, one can see the impressive skyline of Kuala Lumpur—imposing skyscrapers in shiny glass, chrome and steel, with bubble lifts bobbing up and down; the imposing KL Tower, one of the tallest in the world; and the KL City Centre Twin Towers, also amongst the world's tallest buildings. Sleek electric trains cruise noiselessly along elevated tracks, lending a futuristic look to the city. Along the roads ply an incredible number of expensive luxury cars.

But zoom in a little closer and you'll find that things haven't really changed much. Tinted mechanical glass windows of sleek limousines glide down and manicured hands nonchalantly ditch rubbish out of car windows. Yuppies clutching mobile telephones to their ears strut about yelling into their phones. Zoom into the toilets and *aaarrrggh!* ... it still looks like we're back in 1995! The public toilets are filthy, with bits of sodden tissue paper strewn all over the place.

Step into the streets and you almost get knocked down by irate impatient drivers. The driving habits of Malaysians have still not improved, if not worsened in the mad rush to make more money in the name of progress. Drivers are still hogging the yellow boxes, cutting into queues, and honking rudely. Motorcyclists weave in and out of traffic and pedestrians still jaywalk. The super-duper electric trains whiz in and out of stations, leaving the disabled sadly behind in the 21st century.

This scenario is of course just hypothetical, for who can predict the future? Sometimes it seems the things that are difficult to achieve are achievable and what seems relatively easy to achieve can turn out to be the most difficult of all.

While there does not seem to be any doubt that we can achieve progress, in terms of physical and economic development, the mental, intellectual and spiritual development of Malaysians must not be left behind. This concern that we should develop as a nation of all-rounders is articulated in Vision 2020. But often, when we talk of Vision 2020, it seems as if the only concern is that development is measured in terms of buildings, buildings and more buildings—offices, shopping malls, condominiums, hotels, golf courses, housing estates and townships.

Physical development is forging ahead. What about the development of the Malaysian character?

We must take care that in the year 2020, if we do indeed achieve a developed nation status, the people that populate it must also behave accordingly. Generally, Malaysians have a number of bad habits that must be gotten rid of. Here, in my view, are some of the more glaring ones:

Littering

We just can't seem to outgrow this filthy habit. If you visit the home of a Malaysian, it is generally rather clean and neat. But once in public territory, we have this strange mentality that all the world's a dumping ground. Just visit the shopping malls, shops, parks, playgrounds, and other public places and you'll find litter and vandalism everywhere.

What I find most infuriating is that our picnic spots, our streams, waterfalls, beaches, nature trails and forests are clogged with rubbish. If people can seek out lovely restful places for aesthetic relief, surely they should automatically know how to value their beauty without soiling the place.

Even cats know how to cover up their faeces, so why can't we get rid of our man-made waste by throwing it in the dustbin? And if there are not enough bins around, what is so difficult about taking the litter with us until we find a place to dispose of it? Why do Malaysians find it the height of painful embarrassment to have to carry their own litter?

110

Bad driving habits

Of what use is it if we boast about our soaring GDP, zero unemployment and low inflation rate, but still have one of the world's highest rates of road casualties? Why have we this Jekyll-and-Hyde complex once we are on the roads? We talk about the gentle, caring hospitable Malaysian character but this certainly is not the case when we are on the roads, where we transform into rude and selfish monsters.

In the year 2020, with prosperity and development spilling out of our system, are we still going to drive about the way we do now, spilling guts, killing, maiming, never knowing the pleasures of simple road courtesy?

"Tidak apathy"

Malaysians like to pride themselves that they are a tolerant lot. There is a difference between tolerance and sheer *tidak apa* indifference. Generally, we do not speak up enough on social issues and on things that go wrong, leaving the task to "others" to do the job.

"What?! Blast Batu Caves for its limestone? Crazy-ah? Of course, I don't agree! But ... er ... what did you say? You need my signature and I.C. number for your signature campaign? Er, I'm sorry. You know-lah ... I don't want to get involved."

"What? You need my signature to save Penang Hill? I support your cause but ... er, leave me out. I'm scared of getting into any trouble-lah."

These are just two typical responses of *"tidak apathy"*—not being caring and courageous enough to stand up and be counted. A developed nation in the year 2020 needs citizens of courage and calibre, not just cruisers sailing along with the high tide. We should not be afraid to learn the good things from other developed nations, East or West. If one visits the developed nations, one will be impressed at the qualities and mannerisms displayed by the people. Drivers slow down and allow you to cross the road, drivers yield, civic-mindedness and courtesy are generally the norm, parks and public places are clean and well-maintained, and there are plenty of facilities for the disabled.

It is therefore pertinent to be reminded that development must take place on all fronts. To be truly developed, we must shed our bad habits, and mature and flower in all aspects of our lives not only physically but culturally, intellectually, spiritually, mentally and emotionally.

30. THE UGLY 'KIASU'

IF you think that *kiasuism* is a trait peculiar only to Singaporeans, think again. It lurks within the Malaysian psyche as well. And from the look of things, *kiasuism* is on the rise in Malaysia, particularly amongst the educated middle and upper classes of society.

Kiasu literally means "scared to lose" in the Hokkien dialect, and is used to describe those who are afflicted with the "one-upmanship" syndrome. The *kiasu* person must always be one up on his neighbour, friend or relative. If So-and-So has something, then the *kiasu* must also have it, and if possible, bigger, brighter and better. The *kiasu* must always win because he cannot bear to lose! Not that he fears losing, just that he's afraid to be second best.

Kiasuism Malaysian-style manifests itself mainly at certain places and in certain contexts. The best place to find *kiasus* is at high teas at posh hotels where the spread is served buffet style and food can be consumed as much as one likes. Here, you'll find *kiasus* in full force, piling their plates with heaps of food, and going back for more and more. Even if the *kiasu* can't finish the food he's amassed on his plate, he's still got to have that portion of bread pudding, the fried chicken wing, the chocolate mousse or a chunk of whatever he hasn't taken. After all, one has paid a 'fortune' for the high tea and when one pays that much, one's got to make sure one eats for all of one's worth, even if one falls ill in the process!

Some *kiasus* even strategise—skip breakfast and lunch, they say, so that there'll be ample space in the stomach for the high tea! Other *kiasus* advise: "Don't go for the sweets so quickly, *Bodoh*! Stay away from the *Bubur cha-cha* ... *alamak*! ... not so fast! Go for the savouries first so that you won't become so saturated that you don't have space for the savouries later! Like that also must teach you-aa?!"

113

Another useful *kiasu* tip is: "Arrive just when the high tea starts so that you'll have the best of everything, and leave when they're about to close—that's called value for money!"

Another place where you can encounter the Malaysian *kiasu* is at the parking lot. They will drive round and round looking for a parking bay nearest to the shops or entrance. Never mind if there are ample parking lots further away, the *kiasu* has got to find a parking lot that would mean that he gets to walk just that little less. If he can't find a place suitably near enough, well then, he'll just double or triple park, never mind if others are inconvenienced as long as he isn't.

Kiasuism has resulted in some real eyesores in some of the newer housing estates. If the neighbour is renovating his house, why then, the *kiasu* must also do the same. He doesn't quite care about the overall harmony and blending with the environment, as long as his house out-shines the others! If the neighbour's house has four arches, then his house must have eight arches for the patio and since one is at it, why not throw in some Grecian and Roman columns, English bay windows and Spanish hacienda balconies as well! Ever come across houses like that? They scream of cash and crass in their design but lack concept and class. A man's home is his castle, so goes the English proverb, but some of the gargantuan concrete castles that have been built seem like anything but home, and look more like *kiasuism* gone berserk.

The *kiasu* is the one who's got to give the fish the extra poke in its dead flesh just to make sure it's still fresh, the one who's got to scan every apple or pear prodding it for its firmness, the one who must forage the very bottom of the pile of clothes at a sale just to make sure he hasn't missed out on anything. At restaurants, witness the *kiasu* in action at the end of a meal when the bill comes along—he must scan the bill to the n-th degree to make sure he has not been charged for the peanuts which he didn't eat or the towels which he didn't use.

Kiasus also have their antennae up perpetually so as to gauge how other people's children are faring in school, who's getting what tuition and where the best tuition teachers are. If somebody else's child scores more distinctions than the *kiasu's* child, the poor child will get no end of nagging and griping from his *kiasu* parents. "So-and-So's daughter got four As for her UPSR, and you only got three! How am I going to show my face", the *kiasu* parent will moan.

Some say *kiasuism* is a positive trait—a search for improvement in one's life, a quest for being better than others. I say it is not. It's 'keeping up with the Joneses' taken a step further. It's ostentatious, unnecessary and frankly, ugly.

31. COMMON BOND WITH THE ENDANGERED SPECIES

I never thought that I would one day have something in common with the Sumatran Rhinoceros, the Dugong, the Clouded Leopard or the Duckbilled Platypus. But it does seem as though I have. The common factor is that we all belong to species that are endangered. Unlike the animal species though, there's still quite a number of my kind around whereas the number of these animal species is fast diminishing.

I am of Peranakan descent, belonging to a unique cultural group that is approaching the twilight of its existence. Being a Peranakan or a Straits Chinese does have its perks sometimes. Why, I'm even a walking conversation piece. At functions where one encounters foreigners, they are intrigued and cannot quite place me because of my features, colouring, Chinese-name-but-cannot-speak-Chinese-well, etc. Then I have the greatest time telling them about the origin of the Babas and Nyonyas (also known as the Peranakan). And like Scheherazade, I spin them the true story of how in the 15th century, the Emperor of China sent his beautiful daughter, the Princess Hang Li Po, to the court of Malacca to wed the ruler of Malacca, Sultan Mansur Shah. The Princess was escorted by an entourage of five hundred youths of noble birth. Her followers and her settled down in Malacca on a hill called Bukit China, a piece of prime real estate today.

The other less romantic story of the origins of the Babas and Nyonyas was that many centuries ago, the Chinese traders who settled in Malacca, once a thriving and prosperous kingdom, were unaccompanied by their women. Many married the local women here and thus evolved this unique culture which has a blend of Malay and Chinese elements. When two different cultures come into contact, the dominant culture usually takes over and members from the smaller cultural group become assimilated into the larger cultural group. The fascinating thing about the Peranakan community was that this did not take place. Instead, a distinctively different culture evolved, synthesising elements from both Malay and Chinese culture and merging into something which set it quite apart from the two original root cultures.

The Peranakan culture is essentially Chinese in form and Malay in essence. While Peranakan names are Chinese and the Peranakan cling to their Chinese identity and traditional Chinese rites and rituals, they speak a form of Malay patois with many Hokkien words and a sprinkling of English words. The Nyonya dress is essentially Malay, comprising the *sarung* and *kebaya*, a beautifully embroidered garment made of fine voile and fastened together with the *kerongsang*, a three-brooch jewellery item. Traditionally, the Nyonya's hair was combed up into a *sanggul* (a coiled bun) neatly held together with ornate hairpins, and on her feet, she wore a pair of *kasut manek*, beaded slippers painstakingly embroidered by hand. Perhaps the best-known element of the culture is the exotic and tasty Peranakan food, a delightful blend of Chinese and Malay cuisine, with its spicy, piquant taste, its ingredients ranging from *tow cheow*, pigs' liver, mushroom, bamboo shoots, to *serai*, *lengkuas* (galingale), turmeric, chillies and *pandan*.

Today, the Peranakan culture is slowly but surely disappearing. At its height during the 19th to the first half of the 20th century, the Babas and Nyonyas mainly intermarried within their own community, frowning on marriage with other races and indeed even with what they termed the 'China-born' Chinese, that is, non-Straits Chinese. Such demarcations are not strictly observed anymore. The modern Nyonya of the 1990s is a liberated woman, free to make her own choices, freed from a patriarchal social structure which confined the fairer sex to a protected position in the home where she excelled as the homemaker and chef extraordinaire. However, with emancipation, much of the culture is also being discarded and lost. The Second World War and the Japanese Occupation of Malaya also dealt a severe blow to the Peranakan community and hastened its decline and disintegration.

The more the Peranakan culture disappears, the higher the value placed on all things Peranakan. Thus, it is a strange and hair-raising feeling to see the cutlery, crockery and furniture of my childhood fetching prices that are getting more and more astronomical by the year. Grandma's blue-and-white 'batik' bowls which Mama used to serve the most divine *assam laksa* in can now command hundreds of ringgit a piece. Those dainty porcelain spoons with which we used to eat the *koay ee* or glutinous rice balls during festivals now fetch about a hundred ringgit a spoon. To think that we actually broke them quite nonchalantly in those days.

And, of course, the beautiful pink-and-green Nyonyaware with the phoenix and flower motifs which Grandma and Mama used for ancestral worship once a year would cost quite a tidy sum today. I remember how we carried quite casually the whole set of porcelain on a big enamel tray from the kitchen to the front hall to set the table for prayers and back again after. One careless slip and CRASH, the family's entire Straits Chinese crockery legacy would have been wiped out. Through the years, the patterns on the Nyonyaware were gradually fading as a result of constant use. Realising their value, I managed to convince Mama one Chinese New Year to stop using them and keep them—not to be sold but as family heirlooms to be handed down the generations. I went out to a department store and bought her a set of blue-and-white Japanese plates, bowls and spoons to use instead, for the annual ritual on the eve of Chinese New Year. For this important Peranakan ritual, a table was laid with food and prayers were offered to remember and pay homage to our ancestors. I felt quite pleased that at long last, the porcelain were in safe keeping but Mama fretted that somehow the table didn't look quite 'right' with Japanese ware. The spirits of my ancestors must have been even more perturbed—Japanese!

We didn't have much Straits Chinese furniture. My grandparents got rid of the lovely antique living room set they owned many years ago. I remember it was of solid rosewood with handwoven wicker seats and legs in the shape of lions' paws. Back then, nobody was interested in Straits Chinese furniture and Grandma actually had to pay the garbage collectors to get rid of it. Fortunately, the old Nyonya dresser and the *bah lay*, a modern divan, are still with the family. Antique-loving friends who visit my old family home often drool over the old stained glass windows and Italian floor tiles. The whole house itself could be converted into one of those old world, nostalgia-trip attractions.

Step into the antique shops in Malacca and you can feel the ebbing away of a once great and beautiful culture. So much of the jewellery, furniture and porcelain are being sold away by Peranakan families. Will it all disappear one day or does this current interest in and demand for things Peranakan reflect a resurgence in the culture? It is up to us Malaysians to cherish this unique socio-cultural phenomenon that we have right in our midst, to promote an awareness of it, to preserve whatever is left of it, and to ensure that the Peranakan culture does not suffer the same fate as the Sumatran rhinoceros.

WORD FASHIONS

32. FEELING GROOVY

IF a forty-something wants to *hang out* with his teenage kids and their friends nowadays, and tries to be *in* by using the jargon that he used when he was a teen, chances are they'll think he's speaking in a foreign language!

"Hey, guys! Here's some *dough*. Your Dad's in a generous mood today. What say you if we go spend the *bread* someplace, huh? *Groovy*, yeah?" says the earnest Daddy.

"I say, is there something wrong with you, Dad? Why are you talking funny?" will probably be the reply from your teenage kids.

Although the fashions of the 60s and 70s such as bell-bottoms, miniskirts and platform shoes are *in* again today, the jargon used by the teenagers of that era has definitely died out.

For instance, do you ever hear the word 'groovy' anymore? Once it was commonly used by teenagers for anything that was great, fabulous, out-of-this-world. Paul Simon and Art Garfunkel immortalised it in their song *Feeling Groovy*. Today, if you use the word 'groovy' to young people, you'll probably get strange looks. Even your contemporaries will think you're queer, as if caught in a time warp.

Then there was that interesting connection made between cold hard cash and flour ... The two popular words for money then were *bread* and *dough*, as in, "I've got no *bread*, man." Or, "Can you lend me some *dough*? I'm broke."

A *square* today is a square is a square—meaning a figure with four equal sides. But once upon a time, back in the swinging 60s and 70s, a *Square* meant a person who was a bore, a *Drip*, a prudish sort, one whose hair didn't reach his neck! It was considered *hip* (to be *in*, fashionable) to have long hair (for both sexes), to wear bell-bottoms, miniskirts and *Hot Pants*. If your hair had a centre parting, it was considered real *cool*.

If you were not too conventional nor too puritanical, preferably anti-establishment, then you were *in*, you were 'with the crowd'. And if you were *way-out*, it didn't mean that you were out but that you were really, really *in*!

A little three-letter word that bore connotations of working with soil was very popular. This was the word 'dig'. It meant 'to like', as in, "I really dig you." Or, "Wow! I really *dig* your *pad. Outasite! Way-out!*"

In those days, *pad* wasn't a thing for writing on, but meant one's place, room or apartment.

Grass did not refer to the green stuff growing in your garden, but to Drugs, and *Fuzz* was not what you see on unshaved chins but to the Police. *Birds* did not refer to the feathered and winged variety but to Girls, particularly the sweet young variety!

Getting stoned did not mean that you were the target of a stone-throwing session, but that you were really 'high' on drugs or booze. *Going on a Trip* did not have anything to do with suitcases and faraway destinations, but meant getting high on drugs. And *LSD* did not refer to pounds, shillings and pence but to the name of a notorious drug.

Steam did not mean the vapour that came out of the spout of a boiling kettle, but meant that you were having a great time, as in: "How was the party?"

"*Steam* only, man. Like real."

Just as the word 'Yuppie' was associated with the 1980s, the word 'Hippie' belonged very much to the 1960s and 1970s. To be a *Hippie* did not mean that you had too much flab round the hips but that you did not believe in all the things that a Yuppie today believes in. A *Hippie* also dressed, acted and behaved in a certain way—usually as sloppily, untidily and as unconventional as possible. A hippie liked to *bum* around, to *melepak*—(looks like things haven't changed that much after all), wear flowers in his hair and peace medallions around his neck, and ponder ... no, not about the Stock Market ... but about the meaning of the Universe, and his place in it.

Stock expressions then were "Peace, Brudder!" and "Make Love, Not War". When the movie *Love Story*, starring Ali McGraw and Ryan O'Neil, became a big blockbuster, suddenly every teenager was quoting the heroine's famous words: "Love means never having to say you're sorry."

So, in the words of Bob Dylan, a pop icon of those restless, soul-searching times, "the times, they are a-changing". Yesterday's teenagers are Today's Thirty- and Forty-Somethings, wondering in turn why their teenage kids like to lapse into such incomprehensible jargon instead of using proper, respectable English!

33. KEEP IT SHORT AND SWEET

WHEN a Malaysian says "Let's have some ABC," all he wants is a bowl of delicious ice-cold Ais Batu Campur (another name for Ice Kacang) the short form of which is ABC! Malaysians do have a penchant for shortening and abbreviating things and places that take up too much time, and wear and tear on their tongues. For instance, instead of the rather longish Kuala Lumpur, we prefer to refer to our beautiful city as KL, its abbreviated form.

Just why are we so fond of abbreviating places and things, I wonder? Towns with names that are more than three syllables long or comprise more than just a word are more commonly referred to by their abbreviations. For instance, Port Dickson is affectionately called PD, Johor Bahru JB, Kuala Kubu Baru KKB, Kuala Terengganu KT, and Kota Bahru KB. Kuala Kangsar, the royal town of Perak, is referred to as KK. And when we say PJ, we mean specifically Petaling Jaya, and not Pulau Jerejak.

Interestingly, our hill resorts which comprise three or more than three syllables long have been spared. We do not talk about going off to FH (Fraser's Hill), CH (Cameron Highlands), MH (Maxwell Hill), or PH (Penang Hill), though some of us do occasionally go to GH ... General Hospital, the big one at Jalan Kuantan. The other GH is still referred to as Genting Highlands. Perhaps it's because words like 'Hill' and 'Highlands' sound so cool and restful, that it's always nice to have to say them in full.

Sometimes, if you behave in a certain pattern, you can also end up as an abbreviation! For example, " You are a real KPC-*lah!*" would mean that you're such a *Kay Poh Chee*, a Hokkien expression for a busybody, someone who likes to poke his nose into the affairs of others. In Malaysian English, it's quite possible to borrow expressions from other languages and dialects, abbreviate them and throw them into our colourful brand of English.

Many Malaysians like to refer to his or her mother-in-law as "my M-I-L", usually out of earshot of the M-I-L. Interestingly, fathers-in-law are never referred to as FILs. So far, brothers-in-law and sisters-in-law have not become BILs and SILs, neither are daughters-in-law DILs. It's only the poor mother-in-law that has been shortened.

A few weeks ago, at a Chap Goh Meh dinner, I overheard two friends conversing. Lim was telling Taufique how he and his whole clan had to go back to SP for Chinese New Year. Instantly, my ears pricked up. SP? Gee, that was something new! I was intrigued—here was an authentic example. But just what was SP? Culling from all the Geography lessons I could remember of the towns of Malaysia, I butted into the conversation, KPC-style, and said, "Excuse me, but would SP be Seberang Prai?" Both Lim and Taufique, who come from the North, looked at me, astonished, as if the whole world knew what SP stood for. "My dear, SP stands for Sungei Petani!" I was enlightened. When I left them, Taufique was going on about how he and his whole clan would be going back to BM for Hari Raya.

So why do we love to abbreviate? There must be a reason. I guess in short, the long and short of it is that when it gets too long, make it short.

HIGHWAY HORRORS

34. HARROWING TIMES ON HIGHWAY

BEING a regular user of the KL-Seremban Highway, it can be said that I've become quite accustomed to her face, or rather her ever-changing phases. Roadworks take place so often in all types of manner and form that driving along this highway is like driving an obstacle course.

At one time, one of the most common obstacles along the Highway is the Now-You-See-It-Now-You-Don't Obstacle. There you are driving along, when suddenly ... out of the blue, Aarrgggh! Help! Where's the road gone? Are you seeing double? The road splits into two lanes right in front of your eyes without any prior warning. This is because the authorities are resurfacing as well as widening the road and are doing it part by part. The only trouble is that one never quite knows which part until one comes right upon it. To be fair, there are signboards stating 'Harap Maaf' which means that the authorities say that 'We hope We're forgiven for the inconvenience caused'. However, sometimes, on my more morbid days, especially after almost crashing into the road dividers that spring up overnight, I can't help interpreting the 'Harap Maaf' sign as 'We hope You're forgiven if you crash and go to the Happy Hunting Land beyond'!

Another obstacle was the Driven-To-The-Edge obstacle. I don't mean metaphorically but literally. Whole chunks of road have been carved away to your left and to your right, and so you've got to drive very gingerly along. One slip and you fall into the man-made six foot ravine alongside your car. A plus point is that this is a good time for appreciation of geology as you can observe the beautiful layers of rock and soil formations where the road has been sliced through. But then, you've got to keep those eyes on the road!

Apart from physical obstacles, you will also come across obstacles of the human kind. These are certain types of drivers who use the highway. I shall highlight a few of them. There are the Road Hogs who need no explanation. Then, there are the Heavy Breathers, who zoom up from nowhere and take great delight in breathing down your neck. The Heavy Breather will keep on flashing his lights at you to make way for him, but just as you do so, he chooses that precise moment to overtake you on the left.

At the toll plaza, watch out for the Crab. This is the driver who has a *kiasu* mentality. If he sees that the queue in the other lane is shorter than the queue he's in, he'll think nothing of sidling away sideways and charging into the shorter queue. So when pulling up at the toll, don't just look straight ahead, look to your left and right as well. Watch out for the Wobblers too at the toll booths. These are the scatter-brained types who can't find their toll tickets or loose change and are busy poking and groping about in their car seats resulting in their cars lurching about in a drunken fashion.

The bane of many a single lady driver is the Honker. The Honker usually comes in the form of a male chauvinist truck driver who seems to get terribly excited when he sees a Lady, Female or Anything-in-Skirts driving alone on the highway. Honkers seem to think that highways are macho, made solely by men, for men. Sighting a lady highway user is like sighting an albino rhino. The Honker will honk his horn as loudly as he can as you pass him by, making you almost jump out of your skin. As you try to rearrange your jangled facial expression back to its normal alignment, he will come charging pass you, he and his assistant leering and grinning at you, looking as pleased as Punch. That's when you wish you had a horn that could blast an expletive or two.

Lastly, look out for obstacles of the animal kind. I have seen more animal carcasses than some medical students have seen cadavers. Bloated cows with legs pointing to the sky, dead dogs with spilled guts, flattened frogs, stiffened cats, unidentifiable hairy mounds in various stages of decomposition.

Well, have fun driving.

35. MALAYSIAN DRIVERS

IF you ask a foreigner what his impressions are of Malaysians, chances are you'll be told that Malaysians are warm, friendly, helpful, generous and caring. In short, quite a lovely lot. But if you ask a foreigner or even a fellow Malaysian what he thinks of Malaysian drivers, he'll most likely tell you that they are rude, obnoxious, selfish, aggressive, maniacal to the core!

Just how does one reconcile these two absolutely opposite breeds? How can we be so sane and sweet when our feet are on the ground but once behind the wheel of the machine with one foot on the accelerator, we metamorphose into monsters! Well, not all of us really, a minority of us are quite decent drivers. It's the majority that gives us a bad name.

For instance, have you noticed the almost animal-like, wolf pack behaviour of drivers zooming in for the kill at the traffic lights? This trait can be witnessed at a busy intersection where there's a pedestrian crossing. A few stragglers decide to make a dash across the road although all signs indicate that the lights will go green very soon. All of a sudden, the traffic lights do turn green and immediately the traffic surges forward even though the pedestrians are still in the midst of crossing the road.

I have seen terrified people trapped in the centre of the road, desperately trying to tuck in their tummies, toes and feet as cars, motorcycles and minibuses whizz by them, around them and if they only could—through them as well!

What is it about machines that transform us into a manic obsession with haste and hurry? From a relatively laidback and gentle national disposition, we mutate into tyrants once behind the wheel, blasting at anyone who doesn't take off the instant the traffic lights turn from red to green. You are expected to have *already* positioned yourself into first gear, and woe betide you if you are just about to begin the process of doing so.

On a three- or four-lane highway, it's not unusual to find that the longest column of cars is on the foremost right lane when it ought to be on the foremost left lane, the lane for slow traffic! There are many drivers who, no matter how slow, seem to think that they're going fast, and therefore justify being on the right-most lane. This results in a ludicrous situation where the lane for fast traffic becomes the most congested lane and the lane for slow-moving traffic becomes the fastest lane to move along!

Some drivers will think nothing of zooming nonchalantly along the road shoulders and lay-bys, whizzing past scores of cars patiently queueing in a mind-numbing, nerve-wracking jam. And when they have reached the front of the queue, they cut into the queue just as nonchalantly, without a tinge of conscience for those who have been waiting patiently.

If you think that the pecking order is just a bane that you've got to put up with at the office, well, think again—it operates on our roads as well. If you're driving a small car, and you're in the way, buzz off, I'm driving a bigger one then yours. If yours is a 1.6c.c., well, too bad ... mine is a 2.0c.c., so get out of my face fast, before I drive you off the road. And if you are in a beauty of a car, well, I happen to be at the wheels of a huge truck, so get out of my way, for as the statistics show and as is so often quoted in the papers, "the driver of the truck escaped unhurt".

However, it is mind-boggling that all this rush and haste are forgotten the moment there is an accident or a breakdown or a slightest deviation from the normal scenery (it could even be two persons arguing over an accident), then, instantly, the brakes are slammed on, everyone stops and stares, craning their necks wondering why everyone else is doing so, causing massive traffic jams.

If it is a fatal accident, motorists will stop and gawk, look out for the dead body and thank Providence that it's not theirs. The gamblers will stop and take down the registration numbers of the mangled cars to buy at the nearest *Empat Number Ekor* counter. Then off we drive, a little more careful and considerate at first, but with each passing kilometre, the memory of the awful accident gradually recedes and the old jungle kill-or-be-killed instincts emerge again.

We are a rational, reasonable lot. Why is this rationality lost so easily once we are on the roads? A very simple reason is that Malaysians have extremely poor road habits and road discipline. Faced by so much ill-bred driving, even the good drivers deteriorate and pick up the bad habits in order to survive. And thus, every bad habit is reinforced till it becomes part of our character on the roads.

This irrational behaviour shaped by habits can be changed. Long-term measures are through education in schools and road safety and courtesy campaigns through the mass media. For the immediate present, the only way is by force. It is therefore timely that the police are doing their utmost to curb bad driving and bad road habits. Inconvenient though they may be, the spy cameras, the constant police checks, the clamps—they all play a part towards gradually eliminating the callousness we display towards human lives on the roads. Also, road conditions have to be improved by the authorities concerned to reduce stress on drivers which leads to bad driving.

Then, perhaps one day—dare we hope?—Malaysian drivers will become just like what Malaysians generally are—kind, gentle, friendly and caring. Otherwise, having super six-lane highways and sleek, gleaming limousines in the year 2020 will be just a facade of a so-called developed country, when the people behind those wheels still drive around with that same underdeveloped and uncivilised mentality.

36. THE HIGHWAY FLASHER

THE word "flasher" used to have very negative connotations in my schoolgirl days. It conjured images of sick, depraved men lurking around the toilets of girls' schools, waiting for that momentous instant when they could expose their all and sundry to innocent schoolgirls who would then run away, screaming in disgust. But, not so today. The word "flasher" now has positive connotations. I keep a weather eye out for the flasher while driving along the highways and byways. Being a regular user of the Kuala Lumpur-Seremban highway, the flashers of the highway do help keep me on the right track and on the right side of the law.

Well, what is a highway flasher? It simply refers to a motorist who flashes his lights to warn oncoming vehicles that there's a police speedtrap somewhere further up the road. Yes, even amongst the much-maligned Malaysian drivers, castigated for being rude, uncaring and selfish, there exists a common bond—a brotherhood of motorists, you and me and us ordinary folk against the establishment, in this case, the cops. When motorists driving along one side of the highway see the lights of a vehicle on the other side flash, their built-in antennae are instantly put on red alert. A few more vehicles coming along on the other side, flashing their lights and that's it—*Alamak*, speedtrap-*lah*! *Cepat*, switch to the left lane, or rather, *perlahan-perlahan*—let's start crawling, man!

From a situation where cars, lorries and buses are zooming along at breakneck speed all hogging the right lane, these vehicles will scuttle to the left, and if there's no more space, centre lanes, crawling along in the meekest manner possible as if they were the most conscientious drivers on earth! I find this scenario one of the most comical sights alive and an example of Malaysian idiosyncrasy at its most hilarious as well as ludicrous. Buses and lorries which, just a while ago, were trying to mow down anything in their way, now inch along the left lane, chug-chug-chugging as if they could hardly move.

Cars speeding along at 120km per hour, now crawl along painfully at half the speed. All will take part in this great act of observing the speed limit to its most sacred decimal point until such a time when the police roadblock is finally reached. Even those who were not exceeding the speed limit in the first place find themselves slowing down to a snail's pace, for suddenly they get the uncomfortable feeling that they seem to be the fastest ones on the road! The rightmost lane stretches out quite empty—nobody wants to be caught on it!

When the roadblock is finally reached, everybody slows down even more, each trying to outdo the other as the most angelic driver this side of the equator. The policeman whose job it is to flag down the vehicles, stands there looking quite peeved, his red flag hanging limply. The expressions on the faces of the police seem quite resigned—it's all part of the job—sometimes the cat wins, sometimes the mouse. Some unsuspecting drivers—the 'blur ones'—do get caught, unaware of the warnings of the flashing fraternity on the other side.

And once beyond the roadblock, engines are revved, feet clamp down on accelerators, the shining halos are discarded for horns, and Wheee! away the cars, buses, coaches and lorries go again, back to the original scenario before the blinding flashes started.

The other day, as I was driving along the highway, suddenly, just ahead of me, there was a police roadblock. I wasn't stopped as I, ahem ... if you don't mind, always try to observe the speed limits. Still, I found myself feeling cross, my confidence shaken.

Hoi! You guys on the other side—whatever happened to the I-watch-out-for-you and you-watch-out-for-me unwritten code? Why didn't you flash and warn us fellas on this side? What's so difficult about twitching the toggle? Can't one even fraternise on anything anymore? Talk about uncaring motorists ...

I've often wondered why the cops don't use some lateral thinking and catch the real speeding culprits. It's really quite easy—just set up another speedtrap immediately after the first one. After the speed maniacs have passed the first roadblock, they will start speeding mania-cally again and that's when the second roadblock comes in handy.

As for the flashers, don't mind them. They are just kind, consider-ate souls bonding with their fellow brothers and sisters on the road in the most caring of ways!

MALAYSIAN NAMES

37. WHAT'S IN A NAME?

IN *Romeo and Juliet*, Shakespeare says,

> *"What's in a name? That which we call a rose*
> *By any other name would smell as sweet."*

I'm afraid I'll have to disagree with the wise ol' bard on this. English names may smell quite sweet one way or the other but in a country like Malaysia, with its myriad cultures, languages and dialects, you've really got to tread very carefully when naming your child. What may sound perfectly fine in your dialect may take on a different hue or meaning in another dialect or language. Things may be quite cosy for the first few years of your child's life but when he goes to school and meets the whole spectrum of Malaysian society there, that's when you'll know whether his name is 'childproof' or not.

Children are playful creatures—they love to play with anything and everything, including playing with sounds; if they can play with the sound of someone else's name, they will. And if they find that they can distort or contort the name to a different sound or a different meaning, they will too. So, if your sweet little angel, whom you named 'Soh Ai See' (assuming that your surname is 'Soh') comes running home from school one day with tears in her eyes— it could very well be that the little horrors at school have been mangling her name and are calling her 'So Aiksy' or 'So I See'.

The Chinese meaning of the name 'Ai See' could be a beautiful one; 'ai' meaning 'love' and 'see' meaning 'silk'; hence the name could mean 'a love as ethereal as silk' or 'a silken love'(there are of course other meanings depending on how the words are written in Mandarin). However, when it becomes 'So Aiksy', a combination of English and Malaysian English, it means 'She's Such a Show-off', and 'So I See' is English for ... er ... well ... 'So, I See'.

Malaysian Chinese names are at a greater risk than Malay, Indian or Eurasian names. This is because Chinese names comprise three syllables (including the surname) which can be permutated into millions of combinations. An Indian name like Santana or a Malay name like Azizah also comprises three syllables but it's harder to play on such names as they come in a whole entity ... although Santana could still end up being called Santan (the Malay word for 'coconut milk').

Thus, if your name is 'Yong Mo Tuck', you could find your friends calling you 'Yang Botak' ('The Bald One')! And if your name is as ordinary-sounding as 'Seng Ah Song', some kid might call you 'Sing-a-song'! I know a girl, Tan Tse Lee, who was quite happy with her name until she reached the sixth form and went to a coed school and got called 'Darn Silly' by the darn silly boys there.

A good friend of mine named Kong Beng is affectionately called Goat by his friends. This was because he was nicknamed twice—his friends called him 'Kambing' for a while at school, and then a switch from Malay to English, and he ended up with the name 'Goat'. Today he is a successful and well-known surgeon, and known as Dr Khoo by his patients and colleagues, but Goat he is and always will be to the guys who knew him at school.

Another example of names 'going astray' is this incident. I remember my brother coming home from his first week at secondary school one day chuckling away. When asked why, he said that the teacher took attendance every morning and there were two boys in his class named 'You Ken Fatt' and 'Soh Kien Ai'. The trouble was that she called the two names in that order and the two boys happened to sit together, making the boys in class howl with laughter for it sounded like an ongoing flatulence contest.

Of course, there are some parents who deliberately give their children unattractive names. This is not because they don't love their children. It is simply because of the fear that spirits will harm the child that superstitious parents decide to give their child an ugly name, hoping that the spirits will be repelled. Thus, I have two uncles who are brothers, in Penang who are called 'Oh Kow' (Black Dog) and 'Pek Kow' (White Dog). The names don't sound so bad in English but 'Oh Kow' and 'Pek Kow' sure sound scary in Hokkien. I wonder if my Grandaunt, the mother of my two uncles, ever had a 'Beware of Dogs' signboard outside her house?

A long time ago, when I was a child, we had a neighbour who gave birth to a beautiful baby girl. Fearing that the spirits would be jealous, she named her daughter Big Nose ('Tai Pei'). Her second daughter she named Big Thighs (also pronounced 'Tai Pei' but with a different intonation). It must have been difficult in those days for mothers to have to create such names for their children but with infant mortality so high and superstitious beliefs so rife then, their only concern was the child's survival, never mind the name.

But, ah … methinks, I have digressed … as I was saying, do be careful when naming your kid. Pronounce the chosen name many times, look out for any insidious latent permutations hidden within the name, try saying it in several different languages and dialects (that is, if you know any), gargle it about in your mouth, twirl it around with your tongue, and then only pronounce it safe and parent-tested. Then give the whole matter a rest. And if your kid comes home one day and complains that his or her name has been 'nicked', well, at least, you know you tried your best.

Who knows? The kid might just grow to love his nickname.

38. NAMELY OBSERVATIONS

HAVE you noticed that generally speaking, Malaysian names seem to be getting more and more attractive and imaginative? Many of the names given to the younger generations today are quite delightful. A good place to listen to such names is at the waiting room of a paediatrician's clinic. Just listen to the nurses calling out the names ... the names do sound somewhat different from those of just two generations ago.

You'll observe that there's a discernible trend in the way we are naming our children. Names today sound more melodious, more exotic and more ethnic. From Mat, Dollah and Minah, you now come across exotic Malay names like Shafizamra, Nurliza, Rosalina, Karina, Roxanna, Mona Lisa and Puteri Lily. Then, there are the exotic Z names like Zulaika, Zahara, Zurina, Zabedah and Zabarina. And beautiful international-sounding names like Athira, Anastasia, Ramona, Nadia, Natasha and Delilah.

Within the Indian and Singhalese community, instead of the more common names such as Samy or Param, I've come across lovely and more uncommon names such as Prashan, Previn, Pangkit, Arjuna and Roshan.

As for Chinese names, rarely will Chinese parents name their child 'Ah-something or other' today, such as Ah Kow, Ah Kek or Ah Beng. Instead, you'll come across lovely Oriental gems such as Mei Shern, Yu-pin, Pei Min, Zen Lyn, Jie Wei, Ew Jin, Sheao Tsen and Yen Ling. If you listen to the Malaysian Chinese names, there seems to be an almost palpable yearning to be in touch with one's ethnic origins, particularly amongst the English-educated middle classes. The 'pin yin' system of spelling has also resulted in very exotic oriental-sounding names such as Jia Xiong, Wern Jer, Xian Qing, Qi Qian and Xi Li. Do not be surprised that in the near future, when this present generation grows up and starts signing credit cards and forms, initials such as XYZ, QXX, YJX or QQQ might become quite common.

I remember a very interesting fad back in the 70s, pertaining to names. Quite a number of adolescents at that time were fond of giving themselves English, American, French, Italian or shall I say Western names ... not one but a whole string of them! Somehow, this particular category of teens was extremely fond of radio request programmes, and thus one could hear a plethora of names in their full glory on these shows. I can still recall the poor deejays uttering mouthful after mouthful of names, names and names, with hardly any time left to spin the music. Here's a snippet of how the request programme and the names sounded like ... (the words within parentheses are not the words of the deejay but are my explanatory interjections):

"And now, Winnie Wendy Vicky Wong would like to request this song for Engelbert Humperdinck Elvis Gan, with this message 'Keep smiling always!' ... and here's another request from Vincent Valentino Raymond Lum who would like to dedicate this song to Simon Sebastian Ivan Ho and Humphrey Humperdinck Horace Lee, and this song also goes to Faustina Regina Virginia Lim (must be the influence of Barbara Cartland) from a secret admirer, with the message 'Thinking of You ... Always' and here's a postcard from er.. am I reading this correctly ... ah yes ... Lam Seng Beng (sounds positively undressed in such company) to his sweetheart Serena Sindy Sandra Soo, with the message 'Be good and Don't Do What I Won't Do' and here's a request from Dustin Melvin Kennedy Cheong to all his classmates in Form Three F, especially the girls, with the message 'I love you all, and Wishing you Blue Skies and Everything Nice' ... and ... ah yes, and finally the song ... 'Knock Three Times'!"

If you listen to the request programmes today, you'll notice that this penchant for an avalanche of names attached to one's surname has died off. In fact, it's the reverse now. The teenage gals and guys today like to give themselves short, cutesy, snazzy little numbers; the more Pan-Asian sounding, the better, such as Dee, Mae, Lynn, Zoe, Zul, Zal, Sam, Imm, Kai, Kit and Leon. There are also names that transcend the various ethnic groups in Malaysia and are used by Malays,

Chinese, Indians, Portuguese, Eurasians, Kadazans, Ibans, Bidayuhs, etc. Some of these names are Ruby, Anna, Rosediana, Diana, Hannah, Susanna, Sara, Elina, Jasmine, Katerina, Jeannette and Desiree.

All in all, Malaysian names—their origins, their development, their changing trends and patterns, their meanings, their geographical distribution—make for fascinating study. Perhaps, someday someone out there will record them for posterity.

YESTERYEAR MEMORIES

39. MEMORIES OF GOOD OL' NEW YEAR DAYS ...

IT is just two weeks to Chinese New Year, and yet my kitchen lies empty. The sights and sounds, the hustle and bustle, the frantic spring-cleaning and full-scale cake-making that I associate with preparing for Chinese New Year have not commenced yet in my home. All I have managed to do so far in terms of preparation for the New Year was to nip down to town after work yesterday, head for the grocery shops opposite the Central Market and there spend some happy moments buying stuff like dried longans, lychees, mushrooms, gingko nuts, bamboo shoots and some other ingredients. They are now stashed away in the larder and the making and baking of things for Chinese New Year have still not started.

I think to myself . . . ahh, how easy it would be to just nip away for the New Year and be spared all the hassle and frenzied preparations. I know of many couples, particularly DINKY (Double Income, No Kids) couples who plan to do just that—sign up for a package tour, go someplace nice and then come back when all the fuss is over. Although I have thought about it, I have never done it, and have faithfully celebrated every Chinese New Year at home.

Perhaps it's because deep down inside, I believe that traditions (if not all of them, at least the important ones) should be passed down through the generations. Or, could it be because of the wealth of memories associated with the Chinese New Year my parents left me that I am loathe to run away from it?

Chinese New Year, the first day of the lunar calendar, is the most important festival of the Chinese calendar. It falls anywhere between January 21st and February 19th, the date depending on the position of the moon, and thus it varies from year to year. In the past, festivities usually began on the twenty-fourth day of the lunar month with the send-off of the Kitchen God to Heaven, and continued until Chap Goh Meh, the fifteenth day of the first lunar month.

Chinese New Year was celebrated in a big way in my family. Long before the actual day, the work would have already started. A complete spring-cleaning would take place with everyone pitching in to help. New clothes had to be made or bought. The old lace curtains had to be taken down and new ones put up. Walls had to be whitewashed and cobwebs, clinging on high ceilings, swept away.

At least two weeks were devoted to baking cakes and cookies. Mama, a true-blooded Nyonya and a superb cook, would make most of the traditional Chinese New Year delicacies such as pineapple tarts, *kueh bangkit, keropok*, and if she felt up to it, *kueh kapit* (love letters). Although my grandparents and parents have passed away, the memories of Chinese New Year spent with them are indelible. I can still see Mama bustling about in the kitchen, in her red wooden clogs, her arms coated with flour, kneading the flour for the *kueh bangkit* on a huge enamel tray. I can hear the clackety-clack of the wooden *kueh bangkit* moulds as we knocked them against the wooden boards and out would come lovely starch-flour cookies in the shape of dragons, birds and fishes.

The children were assigned the task of putting the finishing touch—a little red dot on each cookie to represent the eye of the animal. How we enjoyed that! Grandma would help by shaving the ends of a few toothpicks to very sharp points. We would dip these into red dye and then dab each *kueh bangkit* with a dot. Too long and hard a dab by a tardy hand would result in an enormous, blotchy red eye on the *kueh*. Grandma would then fish out her *cucuk sanggul* (a pin) from her *sanggul* (hair tied in a bun) and poke the culprit's hand—her way of ensuring quality control.

As Chinese New Year drew nearer, everything took on a more frenzied pace. Ingredients had to be bought fresh from the wet market, washed and prepared. Nothing was processed, blended, freeze-dried or microwaved. Everything was prepared the traditional way. Even the curry powder was home-made, involving a long process of washing, cleaning, drying and milling at the Bangsar mills.

Spices or *rempah* had to be *giling* (blended) the right way using a flat stone slab and a huge stone rolling pin. *Sambal* had to be pounded using the traditional stone pestle and mortar, and the ingredients had to be pounded in the right sequence. Even the pounding motions had to follow a certain rhythm. For example, if you went Tonk! Tonk! Tonk! regularly and consistently, then you were pounding it correctly, but if you went Tonk! Tonk! Tink! Ka-Toinng! Toc! you would get a knock on your head for spoiling the *sambal.*

It was said that the upbringing and culinary skills of a Nyonya could be discerned just by the way she pounded her *sambal.* Fortunately, then, my sister and I were quite spoilt and never had to do the hard labour. Unfortunately, now, because I never took on a 'hands-on' approach, I never quite mastered the technique, and the way I pound my *sambal* would make—as my mother used to tease me—a Nyonya mother-in-law *pengsan* (faint)!

Piles and piles of garlic, shallots and Bombay onions had to be peeled. The vegetables for the *achar* had to be cut—cucumber, carrot, long bean and chilli were cut into tiny, dainty portions, less than an inch long, and two slits were made on every piece so that the *rempah* could seep in. Peanuts were fried patiently over a slow fire, then tossed on the *nyiru* (bamboo tray) to separate the skin from the seed, and then pounded.

To this day, I can still smell the smells, hear the sounds ... I can still picture Mama sitting on a low wooden stool in the *tim chae* (court-yard), a pair of pincers in her hand, plucking away the remaining fine hairs of the duck for the *Itik Tim* soup, a 'must' for all Peranakan reunion dinners. Or standing by the stove, peering into the big *belanga* (an earthenware pot used for cooking curries), stirring away at the *rempah* with a *senduk* (ladle), sniffing the aroma to determine whether it was just right.

I can see Chow Chae, my amah, squatting by the *tempayan* (a big vessel used for storing water), washing the pig intestines spread out over the bottom of a round basket, cleaning them many times for the

Pork Liver Balls dish. And dear Papa, his face beaming with happiness, munching away at the home-made *keropok* (prawncrackers) combined with the *achar*—a delectable combination, enjoying his role as a 'tester' of whatever dish that came off the stove or out of the oven. There were no written recipes. The recipes were all stored in Mama's head and all the ingredients were measured the *agak-agak* or 'guess-guess' way.

On the morning of New Year's Eve, our ancestors would be remembered and honoured. Offerings of food and fruits were made on a table draped with a beautiful embroidered red cloth. Two red candles mounted on antique brass candlesticks, and joss-sticks were lit. Every offering had a little red paper cutting, with intricate patterns, stuck to it. The table would only be cleared after we were sure that our ancestors were satisfied and full. This 'information' was obtained by tossing two coins in front of the table—if one turned Heads up and the other Tails, then it was permissible to clear the table.

The Reunion dinner, a joyous and meaningful occasion, would take place on the eve of the Chinese New Year. Then the house would be thoroughly mopped one last time and after that, no more sweeping or cleaning was allowed. The Chinese believe that sweeping one's house on New Year's day sweeps away one's luck—this custom is still observed in most Chinese homes today.

The nearer it was to the Chinese New Year, the greater the sense of excitement and expectancy. The sound of firecrackers intensified with each mounting hour. We would wake up early on Chinese New Year and dress ourselves in our new clothes. In the quiet of the morning, we observed an important and ancient ceremony. We paid our respects to our parents by kneeling in front of them, and offering them a cup of tea. They would sip the tea and then give us an *ang pow* each and their blessings.

Later in the morning, the house would be a riot of colour and noise. First to drop by would be the neighbourhood kids, fresh and early, to tuck into the New Year goodies and down the fizzy drinks, the customary *ang pow* tucked away in their pockets. Guests would come streaming in steadily, sometimes pouring in till there were no more seats left in the house. There was much laughter, conversation and the rekindling of old ties and friendships. Occasionally, a gambling session (allowed only once a year) would take place, and we had great fun playing Twenty-One, Blackjack and Polish.

We would also go 'Lion hunting'. The moment we heard the sound of the Lion dances, we would pile into the car and with our ears all perked up listening to the sound of the gongs and drums, we would follow the trail of the lion dancers and watch enthralled as they performed. At night, all the neighbourhood kids would come out and play fireworks, firecrackers and sparklers. Some of the driveways and verandahs of our homes would be covered knee-high in red paper, the burnt-out leftovers of long, long strands of firecrackers, strung together and hung on a bamboo pole and it became a matter of pride to have the most 'red' and messy driveway.

So here I am today, the recipient of a rich heritage, nurturing treasured memories ... wondering how with a fourteen-day countdown and a zero state of preparations, I'm going to fit it all in, do it all up, hand them all down? Many Malaysian women are probably in the same predicament. Unlike our mothers and grandmothers, many modern mothers today hold full-time jobs and cannot find the time nor the energy to do what our mothers did. Or have we become a little more pampered, a bit more lazy and spoilt, and a whole load more jaded?

So naaahh, I shall fight the impulse of flying to the beckoning beaches of Phuket or Bali. Surely my child too should have his share of happy memories of the New Year. Like it or not, on the shoulders of women seem to fall the task of transmitting the traditions and customs which we grew up with. In my own way, I shall try and transmit a little of what I so lavishly had. This weekend, I shall dig out the old *kueh bangkit* moulds, and take out the cake tins. My kitchen too shall smell of delicious smells, but unlike Mama, I shall be taking all the microwaveable, processable, freezeable and blendable short-cuts possible.

40. THE ITINERANT HAWKERS OF YESTERYEAR

IF you're feeling a little peckish or downright hungry on a lazy Sunday afternoon but are too lethargic to go out to the shops to get a bite, then the only itinerant hawkers to look forward to these days are the Bread Man and the Ice Cream Man. In most urban areas, cake shops, delicatessens and roadside stalls selling *kueh-mueh* (cakes) and the fabulous *goreng pisang* (banana fritters) abound. But it still means that you've got to drive out in the hot or rainy weather before you can get at the goodies.

I remember, many years ago, on the street where I lived, tucked away in a quiet corner in the heart of Kuala Lumpur, we used to be visited by hawkers galore. Each had his own signature call or signal in the form of bells, horns, or chopsticks knocking on bowls. From morning till night, there was no fear of getting too hungry as one hawker after another would come a-calling.

In the morning, the Yong Tow Foo Man would come by. Steaming hot brinjals, ladies' fingers, glistening red chillis, fat stodgy *tofu* all stuffed with delicious fish paste, served with smooth slithery *chee cheong fun* topped with generous lashings of home-made chilli and sweet *tow cheow* sauces. I loved watching the Yong Tow Foo Man prepare the food, deftly applying the sauces and condiments. When he reached for the bottle of toasted sesame seeds, my sister and I would chorus, "More *chi-ma* (sesame seeds) please." He would oblige and ahh ... what bliss to tuck into such a dish early in the morning.

Come noon, one would hear the tink-tink-tinkle of the Ice Cream Man, whom we called Ah Pak. He sold a wide range of flavours, made at the old Cheong Kee restaurant in Chinatown. His ice cream was sold by the scoop—5 sen per scoop—without any fanciful names or packaging. The ice cream was absolutely superb, particularly the coconut and *jagung* (corn) flavours.

After lunch, the action really started. First came the Tong Sui Man. He sold a variety of sweet soups, usually taken as desserts, such as *Pak Ko Yee Mei* (Gingko Nuts and Barley Soup), *Leng Chee Kang* (Sweet Lotus Seed and Dried Longan Soup), *Hoong Tau Sui* (Sweet Red Bean Soup), Black Bean Soup, *Bubur Cha-Cha,* etc. He only prepared three types a day and would vary his menu from day to day. I was especially happy on days when he sold *Fa Sung Woo* (a delicious groundnut creme concoction) because that was my favourite.

At about the same time, the Fruit Man would come along with his stall of fresh local fruits. He had the most creative signature tune. He would sing out the names of his fruits in Cantonese and in rhyme! He had a loud raspy voice and every kid who lived on that street somehow learnt his jingle by heart. It went something like this: *"Nengka, Nengka, Hoong Mo Lau Lin, Wong Lai eiyah"* which translated, means *"Nengka, Nengka,* English Durians and Pineapples". English Durians? He actually meant the custard apple which looks like the durian without its thorns! The *eiyah* he inserted so that it rhymed with *nengka!*

After the Fruit Man, who would come around the corner but the Penang Rojak Man? Penang Rojak is a mouth-watering salad of mango, papaya, pineapple, radish, bean sprouts, cucumber and *kang kong* (water convolvulus). The Rojak Man would cut the fruits and veggies right in front of you, then mix them all up tantalizingly in a fantastic spicy-sweet peanut sauce in a big porcelain bowl, throw in that all-important *Hae Ko* (prawn paste) before portioning it out.

Later in the afternoon, the Tow Foo Fah Man dropped by. What a treat to tuck into piping hot *tow foo fah* (a hot custardy soya bean milk drink) right at one's doorstep.

The *tock-tock* sound of two chopsticks knocking announced the arrival of the Kon Low Mee Man. *Kon Low Mee* is a very simple dish of noodles seasoned in soya sauce and sesame oil, served with barbequed pork, mushrooms and vegetables. Perhaps it's because of its sheer homespun simplicity that it has an such an appeal.

Occasionally, the Nyonya Kueh Man would walk in. He carried a long wooden pole slung over his shoulder. At each end of the pole was a three-tiered metal container containing an array of Nyonya cakes. Watching him remove each tier was like looking into a treasure chest as trove after trove of colourful *kueh* such as *pulut inti, onde onde, abok abok, kueh talam, kueh bengka, pulut tekan* and *kueh koo* were displayed. The most incredible thing was that, despite his very heavy load, he also sold *Assam Laksa* as well, carrying a huge enamel pot of that fantastic Assam Fish Curry on the same pole!

At around 4:00p.m. another type of Rojak was available—Indian Rojak this time. I can still remember the Indian Rojak Man in his white *dhoti*, with his two red wooden boxes of paraphernalia attached to his bicycle. *Jee Ee* (Second Aunt), whenever she visited, would time her visit to coincide with this Rojak Man, so fond was she of his rojak.

Once in a long while, another Ice Cream Man came by. He had an ingenious way of selling ice cream—with a wheel-like contraption somewhat like a roulette wheel attached to the back of the ice box. Fork out 5 sen and you got a spin at the wheel—if the wheel stopped with the arrow pointing at the number '7' then you got 7 scoops of ice cream! But if it stopped at 0, then of course you got nothing! I guess we kids were already veterans at the *Wheel of Fortune* long before we ever heard of the popular TV gameshow.

Tink! Tink! Tink! The sound of two metal objects hitting each other meant—the Candy Man! He was another favourite. He sold a hard, gooey candy laced with sesame seeds in a round tin tray, which he carried on his head. The candy pieces had to be knocked out with a chisel. For 5 sen, you got a few pieces which you then sucked to your heart's content.

Then, there was the Chendol Man. How we enjoyed watching him prepare the chendol using the traditional Ice Scraper, consisting of a wooden slab in which a sharp blade was inserted. An ice block was scraped over the blade and the ice shavings collected. Then, into a bowl was placed oodles of wriggly green *chendol*, fresh coconut milk, layers of ice shavings and finally, lashings of *gula melaka*.

It's impossible to list them all. There were also Ah Kit, the bare-footed Satay Man, who actually carried on his shoulders all the equipment and ingredients required to barbeque satay in two containers slung on a pole; Ah Ter, the Char Koay Teow Man, who came around on a huge motorbike and fried the *Koay Teow* right at one's doorstep; the Tunghoon Soup with Fishball Man, the Popiah Man ... and depending on the seasons, hawkers selling durians, mangoes and toasted chestnuts came by.

When night descended, all was peaceful and quiet once again on the little street of old pre-war houses. Then as its occupants prepared to go to bed, the roaring sound of burning carbide lamps wafting in the still night air meant that the Char Siew Pau Man was just around the corner. One by one, the verandah lights would come on and the neighbourhood came to life again as its residents, clad in pyjamas, nightgowns and 'housecoats' strolled out to buy supper—delicious *Char Siew* (Barbecued Pork) and *Tow Sar Pau* (Beanpaste Buns), *Loh Mei Kai* (Glutinous Rice) and *Dim Sum*—just perfect for a late night supper.

Where have all these itinerant vendors gone? Except perhaps in the smaller towns, they are rarely seen in the cities. They could never ply their trade today along the cities' congested roads and relentless traffic. Everything has a price tag attached to it. Even Progress. Writing this article has made my tummy go quite rumbly. I hear the tooting of a horn and some shouting outside. Could it be, could it really, possibly be FOOD?

"Paper Lama, Paper Lama! Old Newspaper!" goes the voice. It belongs to the Old Newspaper Man, who cruises around the neighbourhoods collecting stacks of newspapers from households willing to part with them. Alas! While you can recycle old newspapers, you sure can't eat them!

41. THE FORGOTTEN FEASTS OF CHILDHOOD

W HAT is it about fast food that attracts little children so? My son Jan Ming, at four and a half years old, could sing the Kentucky Fried Chicken signature tune by heart and recognise the golden arches of McDonald's no matter what country he was in.

However, I can't stand fast food. Whenever I succumb to Jan Ming's pleas for a meal at a local fast-food joint, I have to force myself to swallow a burger grudgingly, dreaming miserably of Hainanese chicken rice, banana leaf rice or *nasi kandar* which I could have had instead.

There was no such thing as fast food when I was a child. Children nowadays would probably find it inconceivable if you tell them that we never heard of a Big Mac or a pizza when we were young.

What were the foods of my childhood? Well, I can remember the incredible ice ball. For just five sen, the ice-ball man would grate a whole mountain of ice shavings, and using his bare hands, compress them into a huge ice ball, with some corn, *cendol* and red beans packed within. A few lashings of syrup and milk on the ice ball and it was ready for slurping to one's content.

One had to toss it from one hand to the other as it was pretty cold clasping ice. We must have looked pretty unsophisticated sucking away at the ice, tossing the ball around and squealing with delight from the cold, but *mmmm* ... it was simply unforgettable!

My favourite childhood concoction was buttered bread dunked in coffee. First, I would cover a slice of bread with thick slivers of butter. Then, I would fold the slice of bread into half, and dunk it into a cup of thick *kopi-O* (black coffee with sugar).

What dexterity it required to dunk the bread to just the right degree of "dunkness", and then gobble the dunked part before it got too soggy and collapsed into the coffee. At the end of it all, the *kopi-O* looked really disgusting with globs of butter floating on its surface which I would down with the greatest lip-smacking satisfaction.

My mother had an interesting concoction which we absolutely loved. It was a sandwich made of pork rind filling. Whenever she prepared lard, the leftover residue would be the crispy little nuggets of pork fat called *chee yow cha* in Cantonese. She would then sprinkle salt over the sizzling hot *chee yow cha*. They tasted heavenly eaten with bread.

Our *amah* also introduced us to another interesting concoction. She called it the Poor Man's Meal. In China, where she came from, her people were so poor that sometimes there was nothing to eat except white rice. Instead of just rice, what they would do was to pour a dash of black soya sauce on a plate of rice, add some plain boiled water to it, and eat that as a meal. Sometimes, when we were feeling peckish, she would prepare this dish for us, telling us stories of hardship and hunger. Strangely, I remember my sister, brother and I enjoying it very much, perhaps because of its starkness and simplicity.

But I must admit that my favourite childhood food is toasted bread with *kaya* (a jam made from a mixture of coconut milk, eggs and sugar). I write with some nostalgia as it's hard to find this type of bread now. It came in fat loaves with thick brown crusts. They were unlike the sliced sandwich loaves of today; one had to slice the loaves manually with a sharp knife, otherwise the loaf would be pressed out of shape. The slices of bread were then toasted over smouldering charcoal, cut into half length-wise and spread with lashings of delicious, fragrant homemade *kaya*. The *kaya* was really *lemak* (rich)—one could taste the eggs and the coconut milk that went into it—quite a contrast from the sweet and gooey stuff they call *kaya* nowadays!

How will the children of today reminisce about their childhood foods one day, I wonder? It'll probably go something like this: "Aahh ... in the good old days, we used to have to queue for our food at the fast food joints, not like you young people today, instant pill-poppers! And the chicken was finger-lickin' good and the burgers and hot dogs were real great stuff and our parents were *Sir*-ed and *Madam*-ed all the way and told to have a nice day, and the food came in the cutest styro-foam boxes. Aahh, those were the days when food was really food."

42. THE GAMES WE USED TO PLAY

I miss those game chants which we used to chant as children whenever we had to determine who would be 'It' for a game of Catching or Hide-and-Seek. Children nowadays, especially those in the urban areas, don't use these chants very often. I guess growing up in these high-tech times does rub off somehow. Chanting might seem almost primeval!

To determine who would be 'It' for a game in those days, if there were more than two persons, we had to stand in a circle facing inwards and turning our palms upwards and downwards, we would chant in a singsong fashion, *'La-la-li-la-tum-pong'*. The person who was the odd one out (for example, the only one whose palm faced upwards while the rest faced downwards) would exit from the group. This went on until there were only two members left.

Then, they would have to fight it out by doing the One-Two-Zom chant. Facing each other, with their right hands behind their backs, they would go 'One-Two-Zom'. At the count of the word 'Zom', both had to show their right hands simultaneously, with the hands shaped to represent a symbol.

Only three symbols were allowed: Bird, Stone and Water. All four fingers and thumb straightened and pressed together represented 'Bird'; fingers clenched together in a fist represented 'Stone'; and palm flattened out, facing downwards represented 'Water'. Every symbol had a fair chance. Bird lost out to Stone (Bird gets killed when hit by a Stone), Stone lost to Water (Stone sinks when thrown into the Water) and Water lost to Bird (Bird drinks Water). It was great fun just going through these procedures before playing the game itself.

What were the games we used to play? One favourite was 'Police and Thief'. This was also preceded by a chant. All the children playing had to stand in a circle, put out one hand with thumb sticking out and fingers tucked in, and form a pyramid with their hands, fingers clasping thumbs. Then someone would chant the Police chant and Thief chant alternatively, pointing at each clasped hand with each syllable of the chant. At the end of the chant, the last person whose hand was touched would be part of the police squad or the band of robbers. If there were ten persons playing, then the chant would have to be repeated nine times. It took quite some time but it was all very democratic.

The game was played with the police doing what else, the job of chasing and catching the thieves. Once a thief was caught, he was put in 'prison' and his comrades had to try and rescue him. This went on till both sides wearied of being the chaser or the chased, and a switch-over took place.

A favourite game with the boys was a game called 'Chopping'. Each boy had to dig a little hole in the ground, the size of a tennis ball. The holes were all dug near each other in one or two rows. A tennis ball was then rolled towards the holes. As all waited with bated breath, poised to take flight, the ball would careen towards the depressions and slowly tip into one of them. Whoever had dug that particular hole would have to grab the ball and lunge it at the rest of the boys who would all be madly scrambling away in all directons. If he missed, he would get a point against him and a pebble would be placed in his hole. If he had managed to 'chop' someone, then his victim would get a point.

The boy who got the most penalty points after some time had to face a 'chopping' squad. He had to stand against a wall while each member had a chance to aim at him with the ball from a certain distance. Then the game would start anew with a clean slate for everyone.

Other favourites were 'What is the time, Mr Wolf?' and 'AEIOU', which were different variations of 'Catching'. The first game was played with a bunch of children tailing the Wolf and chanting, "What is the time, Mr Wolf?" The 'Wolf' would respond by giving the time such as 'Ten o'clock' or 'Six o'clock'. But when Mr Wolf felt that he had lulled the kids into a state of complacency, he might decide to respond by saying, "It's Dinner Time!" That's when everyone screamed and ran for their lives as Mr Wolf turned around to grab someone for dinner.

Girls played gentle games like *Masak-masak* (Cooking) and games which required dexterity such as 'Hopscotch' and 'Five Stones'. Sometimes, there were seasons and fads—flying kites, spinning tops, playing marbles, and collecting cards, comics or bottle covers. Occasionally, the boys in the neighbourhood would be seen foraging in the bushes and shrubs looking for fighting spiders to pit against each other. During the rainy season, we would squat by the monsoon drain nearby and watch, and try to catch the scores of newly-hatched wriggly tadpoles.

Time moves on and lifestyle patterns change. The childhood of Malaysian kids today in these more affluent and sophisticated times will continue to be distinctively more different than the childhood of earlier times. Without any doubt, the games we used to play and the chants we used to chant will one day become just a memory.

43. THE STORY OF AN AMAH

As a result of the scarcity of local domestic help, more and more Malaysian children are being left in the charge of foreign maids nowadays, when their parents go to work. Most of the foreign maids come from Indonesia and the Philippines. Thirty years ago, the 'black-and-white' amah or maid from China was still prevalent in the domestic help scene. Today, their numbers have dwindled to almost a handful, many of whom would be exceedingly old by now.

They will be remembered as a social and historical phenomenon, a group of young women who came from China to Malaya before independence who chose a certain way of life. They came to work as servants and usually served their employers till infirmity or death. They came not in search of fabulous wealth but in search of their own economic survival, freedom and independence, and in a way, in search of somewhere to belong to.

They came without any family nor did they start any family of their own. They were mostly unmarried, though there were some who came as widows. The 'push' factor from China was usually poverty, hardship and oppression. On arrival in their adopted country, they followed a code of celibacy and dressed in a distinctive manner, a simple white *sam foo* top and loose black pants, hence the term 'black-and-white amah'. Their feet were shod in slippers or wooden clogs, never shoes. Their hair were kept in long plaits if they were spinsters or tied up in a bun at the back of their heads if they were married. They led very simple and frugal lives.

They had no regular off-days, nor any kind of agencies to protect them or fight for their rights. They signed no contracts. They 'lived in' with their employers and worked seven days a week, throughout the year. Occasionally, they took a day-off and they usually visited their association houses or *kongsis* which were located in town. These *kongsis* were called *fong tsai* and were usually rented rooms in old shophouses. There, they would spend the day chatting or 'catching up' with other members of their chosen sisterhood.

Despite the odds against them, in the span of a few decades, they had forged such a reputation for themselves through their industry and reliability that they were much sought after and treated with respect and affection by the families they worked with.

My family had an amah too. Her name was Leong Yee. She came to work with us when my sister, the first child in the family, was born and she stayed with us until her death in 1971. She came from a poor peasant family and was forced at a young age to marry a man suffering from tuberculosis. She had never met him before. On her wedding night, she was pushed into a room where her sickly husband lay, his body racked with coughs, too ill even to get up for his wedding.

He died a few months later and she was blamed for having brought misfortune into the family. Her mother-in-law treated her cruelly. I remember her telling us stories of how she was forced to fetch water everyday from a well a distance away until she felt her arms would break. One day, unable to take the cruelty and suffering anymore, she decided to run away. To run home to her family would be in vain for they would have only sent her back to her marital home. With the help of a friend, she managed to get to a port and boarded a ship to Malaya.

She was not attractive physically. She had a plain face, a stout frame and big coarse hands and feet. But she had a heart of gold, capable of infinite love and a loyalty that went beyond the call of duty. Although her name was Leong Yee, her nickname was Chou Chae and that was what we called her. She addressed my parents and my grandparents with the traditional names that a servant used when addressing her employers. But, she called us, the children, by names as if we were her own. She called my elder sister *Ah Nui* which meant Daughter, my brother *Ah Chai* which meant Son, and I, the second daughter in the family, she called *Ah Mui* which meant Sister in Cantonese.

She had no children of her own. Except for her family which she left behind in China, she had no one. We became her family and she became part of ours. Our joys became her joys and our sorrows hers. When there was a death in the family, she mourned as if she had lost her own flesh and blood. She beamed with joy and pride over our little accomplishments, fussed over us when we fell ill and nagged if we misbehaved.

I remember on certain chilly mornings, when we had to get up very early to go to school, she would iron our school uniforms which had already been ironed the day before just so that we would feel that freshly-pressed warmth. When Mother wanted to cane us with the cane for misbehaviour, we would go running for Chae Chae (that's what we called her), and hide behind her burly physique. She would hold up her arms and try to block my mother's swishes of the cane, acting like a mother hen protecting her chicks, while we giggled and squealed with glee. Mother would give a few token swipes and then give up, pretending that it was an impossible task to do.

Because we were a Peranakan family, we did not know how to speak Cantonese. It was through our amah, Chou Chae, that we gradually learnt how to speak Cantonese. She adapted quickly to life here and soon, could eat our food, learnt our customs and could speak a smattering of bazaar Malay. She even stopped using chopsticks, and ate with her fingers like the way the elders in my family did!

With time, she learnt how to prepare the ingredients for Peranakan cuisine as skilfully as any Nyonya. Although my mother was acknowledged as the supreme chef in the family (my father would not eat anyone else's food but that cooked by Mother), Chou Chae, because of her strength, was the best when it came to tasks like *giling rempah* (rolling and blending fresh chilli on a stone mortar with a stone rolling pin) and *tumbuk belacan* (pounding toasted prawn paste with fresh chllies). When Chinese New Year came along, it was Chou Chae who would knead the flour for the *kueh bangkit* and twirl the *kueh kapit* moulds over the burning hot charcoal stove. On a slight hillslope behind our house, she took to planting *pandan, serai, daun kaduk, bunga kantan* and the curry leaf tree, disapproving of my mother having to spend good money in the market to purchase what to her could be easily grown.

Her lifestyle was exceedingly spartan. She could have bought herself some nice things if she wanted to with her earnings but I never saw her giving in to any form of indulgence. She did not use any powder on her face. She washed herself with soap and water: there were no feminine luxuries such as shampoo, moisturiser, lotions, perfume, nor paraphernalia such as bags, shoes nor stationery. At night, she slept on a blue and white porcelain pillow from China. Only once a year would she buy some materials to make some new clothes for Chinese New Year.

She saved all her earnings and sent some money home to her family once every few months. Sometimes, we would accompany her on her day off to Chinatown where she would look for a scribe to write a letter to send home. These scribes are almost an extinct species now. In those days, they earned a living just through their sheer ability to write in Mandarin. They sat behind tiny makeshift tables under an umbrella or in the verandah of a shophouse and their tools were a brush, a pot of ink and some paper.

Chou Chae would sit on a chair at the table and tell the scribe the gist of what she wanted to say to her folks and he would then write out the letter for her. As none of us knew Mandarin, we never could tell what he had written and had to take his word for granted. But one could tell that the learned man was proud of his trade for after completing the letter, he would always insist on reading it out loud in a stentorian tone, impressing us into a hushed silence with his elegant-sounding prose.

She made a trip home to China once when her parents had grown weak and frail and wanted to see her for the last time. That was the one time when she spent a lot of money buying presents for her family and friends. Her father had written to tell her that his greatest wish was to own a pair of Fung Keong slippers with the straps crossed in the Fung Keong (a local shoe manufacturer) style.

So she made a trip to town and bought a pair of slippers, the straps of which were of a soft, velvety material, specially for her father. She sailed home on a P&O liner, third class, bringing with her some bicycles, small radio sets, watches, old clothes, patchwork quilts and jackets made out of remnant material which she had collected and sewn together, biscuits and other foodstuff.

When she came home from her trip to China, the story she told us moved us to tears. For the whole of her first day home, she was visited by a stream of relatives, friends and neighbours. To them, here was the prodigal daughter returned home, someone who had made it good in a faraway land of rich and plenty. They were grateful for whatever little gift she had for them and they were thrilled by her stories of life abroad. Her father waited patiently in the background waiting for all the folks to leave.

Finally, late at night, the last of the visitors had gone. Tremulously, he waited for his daughter to give him the gift he had asked for. She removed it from her bag and gave it to him. With trembling hands and eyes shining with excitement, he opened it and took out the pair of slippers. Then she saw his expression turn from joy to disbelief to sadness. She looked at the slippers and to her horror, saw that they both were meant for the left foot. The salesgirl had somehow placed in two left-footed slippers and Chou Chae in a rush, had not checked. The old man blinked away tears of sheer disappointment while his daughter wept, aghast at her mistake. After that, the old man never spoke of the matter again.

Life moved on, and she was there at each milestone of our lives. She watched us, the children, grow from infancy to adolescence. Throughout her stay with us, she had seldom fallen ill. Then one day, when she was in her fifties, she felt pains in her abdomen. Tests conducted revealed that she had cancer of the womb, in the advanced stage. We were devastated. She was a part of us, she was family. Servants we could live and function without, but how could we live without her?

She passed away a few months later. I still remember the telephone call from the Universiti Hospital where she was under treatment. I answered the call and heard the voice on the other end: *"This is the ma-*

tron speaking. I'm sorry to inform you that Madame Leong Yee passed away at three this afternoon."

Her body was cremated and all those who knew her and loved her accompanied her ashes on her final journey to a nearby port. There, we took a boat out to sea and sadly, threw her ashes into the all-embracing blue waters, back into the sea that had brought her into our lives in the first place, touching us so richly and profoundly.

44. WHO HAS THE BETTER LIFE?

A pastime which I enjoyed as a child was watching Grandma dress up. This took place in the afternoon after lunch when she would get ready to go out for a game of *chiki*, a popular card game played amongst the Babas and Nyonyas.

Grandma was a beautiful woman, fair, with big, deepset eyes, a high forehead and lovely cheekbones. She was a Nyonya, from Malacca, and was married to my grandfather at the early age of fourteen. Apart from the Baba patois, she could speak Malay, Hakka, Cantonese and Hokkien as well as English, having received some years of formal schooling at the Methodist Girls' School before she was married off.

In those days, the Peranakan community frowned upon girls going to school, fearing that too much education would make them *bebas* (wild). Nyonya maidens were brought up to be good wives and good homemakers and were trained in the culinary and domestic skills from an early age.

I had the feeling that Grandma secretly railed at the system and felt that her potential was never fully realized. This I could perceive from her occasional comments and asides to me.

"If I were born in your time, in your age, why, the things I could achieve ..." or "if only I were of your generation, I could do so much more with my life ..." she would say, not bitterly nor wistfully but with a steel-like sureness of purpose.

When I pressed her and asked her what she envisaged she would have become had she the opportunity and freedom, she replied with a glint in her eye, and with conviction, "I would have become a doctor, or better still, a businesswoman." And she certainly would have been, for she was sharp and shrewd and, despite her limited education, highly intelligent.

In her old age, she led a comfortable lifestyle and liked to while away her afternoons playing *chiki* at a friend's house on the next street. After a bath, she would begin her daily leisurely dressing-up ritual. She would come out of the bathroom *berkemban* (dressed in a sarong tied up at chest level without a blouse or any other covering), and saunter to the centre hall where we usually spent our afternoons.

Standing in front of the antique dresser, and keeping a steady eye on the mirror, she began to comb her long grey hair into a *sanggul* (a coiled bun), the traditional hairdo of the Nyonyas.

She would comb her hair many times, then bend over and gather her hair into a tight ponytail at the top of her head. She then secured a thin hairpiece to the existing ponytail and twirled her hair slowly and carefully into a neat round bun, pinning it down with black hairpins.

As if this was not troublesome enough, she would spend some time stroking whatever stray hair left into the base of her bun, using a long black thread held at each end. Finally, a black net was looped over the *sanggul* and two hairpins tucked in.

She also kept a silver pin (used for clearing ear wax) in her bun, a most convenient place for whenever she found her grandchildren meddling with her things, she would grope for the sharp metal object hidden in her bun and poke the culprit's hands with it, an action which spoke more effectively than words.

After checking out her *sanggul* in the mirror, she would take out one of her many beautiful starched sarongs and slip into it, with the other sarong still on. With the sarong fastened securely around her waist, she then put on an ornate silver belt. The sarong had to be worn just right, with the *pinta* (a section of the sarong where the motif was different from the rest) in front, and the fold neatly tucked in from right to left, with all the hems perfectly aligned.

Next, she put on a cotton lace-trimmed camisole, and with a tug, removed the first sarong. This was achieved without having to step into a changing room, yet not revealing an inch of flesh! The camisole was tightly buttoned down the front, pressing the bosom down. Accentuating one's breasts was frowned upon by the Nyonyas. The traditional Nyonyas wore neither panties nor bras; the little camisole was all of her underwear.

Next, she donned a starched cotton blouse, known as the *baju china*, the "casual wear" of the Nyonyas in place of the more elegant *kebaya* worn for formal occasions. The *baju china* had a front opening, a mandarin collar, elbow-length sleeves and two big breast pockets. My sister and I were given the job of inserting a set of five gold buttons into the buttonholes of the *baju*, and two gold studs for the collar, secured by tiny safety pins, a job which we both clamoured to do!

A few dabs of powder from a square box of hard rock-like powder on her face sufficed as make-up. Sometimes, she dabbed herself with *bedak sejuk*, a form of powder made from dried fermented rice flour. She kept the *bedak* in a glass bottle mixed with a potpourri of *bunga rampai*, jasmine and finely chopped pandan leaves. A few granules were mixed with water into a paste, then plastered on one's face and body, the powder leaving a "cooling" effect.

Finally, slipping some dollar notes into one of her two large pockets, she slipped her feet into her favourite *kasut manek*, a beautiful green pair of embroidered beaded slippers. Then, flinging a large white handkerchief over her shoulders, she sauntered in a dainty *lenggang-lenggang* fashion out of the house, the rustling of her starched sarong whispering behind her.

Sometimes, when I'm rushing about from one place to another, switching from one role to another, and trying to cope with all the demands and responsibilities a modern working woman finds herself saddled with thanks to freedom and opportunity, I think of the languid, gentle pace of life that my Grandma led, and wish that I were born in her time instead!

45. THOSE THREE SPECIAL WORDS "I LOVE YOU"

IT is one of the little ironies of life that while we may blithely say "I love you" to a spouse, or a friend, or a pet, we are not able to say it to the two persons who mean all the world to us. Why is it so difficult to articulate those words, to express the depth of our feelings to our parents, the two persons whom we have every reason to express our love?

This is particularly so for the older generation of Malaysians. We were brought up to love, honour and respect our parents, but seldom are our feelings ever voiced or demonstrated in affectionate gestures in any way.

I have been fortunate. I had two wonderful parents. My father and I were more open in expressing our affection. My Papa was a tall, big and handsome man. He was plump and round, and absolutely adored children. I loved giving him impulsive bear hugs around his big wide stomach, and till I was about sixteen years of age, thought nothing of plonking myself on his lap. While hugging my father came so naturally to me without the slightest of inhibitions, and while I loved him with all the adoration of a daughter, my Asian Chinese upbringing rendered me incapable of ever telling Papa that I loved him.

One morning, it was too late to do so. At the early age of 62, he passed away due to a heart attack. He left us so unexpectedly I never had a chance to tell him how much I loved him.

Was it necessary? Would it really have mattered? Surely he would have known that he was so very loved? Would saying "I love you, Papa" trivialize rather than enhance this complex and inexpressible emotion between Chinese parent and child? The Asian part of me knew and understood that it didn't matter—that while some of the most unnecessary things are spoken inanely and often, some of the most necessary and meaningful are never spoken, and left unspoken forever. The "Westernized" part of me, though, gnawed at me, asking my inner self why I was incapable of expressing something I yearned to say and that would have meant so much to a parent. I resolved that one day, I would tell Mama that I loved her, before it was too late ...

With Mama, touching and expressing one's emotions were even more uncommon. She seldom hugged or kissed me once I was no longer a child. She was the typical Nyonya matriarchal figure, strong-willed and spunky, who showed her love for her children in her actions and deeds. When I was ill, she would touch my forehead, feeling my temperature, her touch a functional one but imbued with a mother's love. She was an incredible lady, quite unforgettable with a sparkling personality. She was good at languages and could spout Shakespeare and English proverbs to our eternal amazement. She had the liveliest wit and the sharpest tongue. My friends lost out to her whenever they engaged in verbal repartee with her. She was also a great cook and had a wonderful zest for life.

She wasn't just my mother, she was also a great friend. Sometimes I longed to reach out and just give her a big hug, but somehow could never do so. Limbs I could move easily but how do you move against a lifetime of norms and practices ingrained in you?

I did it finally one day by giving her a kiss on the cheek in public. It was after the convocation ceremony where I had just been conferred a Master in Education degree. She was standing there outside the Hall, clad elegantly in her *sarung kebaya*, smiling proudly. She had been widowed for three years then and her hair, once jet-black, had turned completely white from the shock of my father's death. I walked right up to her and planted a kiss on her right cheek, and said in English, "Thanks for everything, Ma."

She looked at me in surprise, as if I had overturned some unwritten rule, a brief look ... was it softness? ... flickered in her eyes, then it was gone. She put on her Peranakan mother role, codeswitched into Hokkien and withered me up with one single word:

"Siau-ah?" which in English can be translated as "Have you gone quite mad?"

When she was 66, she had to undergo a gall bladder operation. She had been completely fine and healthy before the operation. After the operation, the terrible Kafkaesque nightmare began. She kept getting jaundiced and operation after operation was performed on her. She had to undergo four operations in eight months. The pain and discomfort must have been unbearable, but she refused to wallow in self-pity, and was cheerful and chatty whenever family or friends were around. The doctors told us the news we dreaded to hear—she had a rare cancer of the biliary system. We didn't tell her, it was as if she knew but didn't want to know.

One day, I was with her at the hospital. The fourth bypass operation had been performed. A kind of tube called a stendt had been inserted into her thin frail body. There were tubes sticking into her and tubes coming out of her. I sat beside her, drained and helpless. We had fought every battle possible to save her, but still, the insidious cancer inside her was slowly taking over. I had no words left to say that morning, only an unspeakable despair. I reached out for her hand and held it, and to my surprise she didn't pull her hand away. She didn't scold me for being mushy or mad. She looked away but she let her hand rest in mine. After that, quite often, when I went to visit her at the hospital, she would reach out and hold my hand.

Eventually, she was discharged and returned home. She hung on valiantly for six more months, able to walk and talk and hold court with the scores of friends and relatives who came to visit her. However, she grew frailer by the day. One morning, she slipped into a coma. My sister, brother and I took turns to watch over her. I was with her when from the depths of her coma, she willed herself into one moment of consciousness, and said softly, "Come together ..." I nodded. I knew what she meant— that she wanted the family she was leaving behind to stay as a family always. I wiped her brow and whispered, "I love you, Mama". Gently, gently, she drifted away ... a last drawn breath, two tears rolled down her cheeks, a wonderful peace settled over her features and she was gone.

46. A LEGACY OF LOVE

IF I were asked what my father's most important legacy was, my answer would be neither property nor money nor other material things. It would be something which cannot be quantified, cannot appreciate or depreciate in terms of cold hard cash, but which nevertheless enriches me in a way that money cannot. It would be his wonderful legacy of love for nature.

How my father loved the sea. At every opportunity, he would book the little chalet at 3rd Mile, Port Dickson, which belonged to his company and we would spend one to two weeks of our school holidays there three times a year. The Harrisons & Crosfield chalets were located on a hillock facing the sea with a *kampung* (village) behind, and we vacationed there often from childhood right up to adulthood.

From a very young age, I was already quite comfortable with the sea. I could swim like a fish, loved the feeling of the sand and mud beneath my feet, the taste of the sea spray, and the caressing touch of the sea breeze. I know the sea in all its moods—glittering with a million jewels in the afternoon sunshine, dull grey in the rain, inky black at night, silver in the moonlight. I learnt about spring and neap tides, the best times to catch crabs and prawns, how to cast the *jala* or net, and where and when to go fishing with our home-made bamboo rods and lines.

I remember an art lesson when I was in secondary two. We were told to draw a picture of the sea. I drew the sea as I remembered it on a sunny afternoon, painting it in water colours with azure blue, light green, a streak of purple, a patch of grey and dark blue near the distant horizon. The art teacher questioned me, "You have it all wrong, my dear. The sea is blue in colour—why is yours in so many colours?" I defended myself—my painting might not be the most beautiful of paintings but it was certainly correct.

"But I'm afraid you are wrong," I replied, "I have seen it in many shades all at once. See, the light greens and blues here are the shallows, the patch of purple is where there is a huge patch of seaweed under the water, the grey is the reflection of a passing cloud and a breeze rippling over the waters, and the dark blue is the deep part of the sea." She walked away, still in disbelief, but perhaps making a mental note that she really ought to go down to the sea again sometime.

Father's favourite pastime was sitting on the sea wall, gazing at the open sea. The most beautiful hour was of course during sunset. Another favourite time was just before a storm when the sea was at its awesome best, its waves rolling in huge swells. We loved watching the rain falling in grey streaks on the distant horizon, then looming nearer and nearer. We would wait till the very last minute, then make a wild dash back to the chalet before the clouds burst on us.

Apart from the sea, Father could not resist waterfalls, streams and lakes. We picnicked often at popular spots such as Templer's Park and Bukit Belachan. Sometimes, after work, he would take us to the Lake Gardens where we would go for long walks round the lake. I remember picking frangipanis once and asking Father what his favourite flowers were, and his reply was, "My daughters are my favourite flowers."

When Father passed away, his ashes were thrown into the sea, free to mix with the elements, free to merge with the sea which he loved so passionately. When I return to Port Dickson, my eyes play tricks on me ... it is almost as if I can see him sitting there on the sea wall, in his simple white T-shirt and black shorts, with that happy and contented look on his face. He was a man who may not have owned millions, but he was in many ways much richer than his contemporaries.

Whatever we experienced in our childhood spills over into the rest of our lives. My siblings and I all love nature and we try our best to pass on this appreciation of nature to the younger generation. It is a difficult task nowadays. The streams in Templer's Park, Sungei Tua and many of the more accessible nature reserves are clogged with rubbish.

And going back to Port Dickson now sickens me to the pit of my stomach.

Condominiums sprout up everywhere without any concern for the aesthetics of the place, or the fact that the beach belongs to everyone, not just the handful who have bought themselves an apartment or two. At my favourite beach, there now stands a huge condominium sticking out like a sore thumb, marring the scenery and blocking one of the best views of the sea as one drives along the Port Dickson road. It would help if developers 'developed' a social conscience.

I brought Kit, my nine-year-old nephew, into the forest the other day. It was the first time he had ever stepped into the Malaysian rainforest. He was a typical urban Malaysian kid, born and bred in the city, spending most of his time walking around shopping malls, and playing video and computer games during the weekends.

It was wonderful studying his reaction—at first, he was scared of the strange sounds and smells of the forest, his toes cringed on coming into contact with the leafy mossy floor, he tripped over the sprawling roots and for a moment, he wanted to go back to the security of cemented, concrete places. It didn't take long though before he got absolutely smitten, playing in the streams, splashing in the waterfall, and now he loves going to natural spots. Yes, nature enriches us in a very special and magical way.

CHILDREN

CHILDREN

47. THE YUPPIE KIDS TODAY

MANY teenagers today, especially the children of well-to-do, successful professionals, are a fortunate lot. Apart from the usual angst over acne, boyfriends, girlfriends, exams, and other teenage problems, teenagers today seem to be more cash-flushed. This is probably because their parents, being well-off, give them a large amount of pocket money and it is not unusual to come across kids today with their own direct line, their own supplementary credit cards and some, their own cars!

An observation of teenagers today is that they've become more brand-conscious, an outcome of being the offspring of a growing affluent class of professionals and entrepreneurs. Thus, one may come across a teenager all togged up in the latest designer items from head to toe. From the things that one wears on one's hair down to the things worn on one's feet, they should preferably be products with exclusive brand names. While there are brand-wearing adults who do not mind if the brand name cannot be seen as long as the product is classy and expensive-looking, teenagers are particular that the brand has to be noticeable, otherwise why pay so much to wear a brand?

Therefore, a hairband shouldn't just be an ordinary hairband—it's got to be 'branded'—preferably a classy brand such as Evita Peroni. To shade one's delicate eyes from the sun, teenagers will think nothing of splurging over RM300 on a pair of Ray Ban or Armani sunglasses. What? Wear a hat? Thanks but no thanks. Sunglasses look more 'cool'.

A wallet has got to be Ocean Pacific or a Bonia, nothing less. And excuse me?—a basket to put one's schoolbooks? Whoever heard of that? Why, baskets are for people who need to go to the market to buy smelly stuff such as fish and prawns. A schoolbag has got to be Reebok or Bodypac. Some really rich kids even go to school with Moschino bags which cost around RM700! Imagine, seven hundred ringgit— the equivalent of the monthly salary of a primary school teacher—just for a bag to put one's schoolbooks in—it's enough to turn a teacher green and contemplate playing the stock market!

As for wrist watches, they've got to be brands like Swatch or Guess, genuine ones, mind you, and not the *pasar malam* (night market) variety. And if Dad or Mum can afford it, a Tag Heuer in the vicinity of RM1,000 would do just fine. Shoes should preferably be a pair of Reebok, Nike or Doc Marten, nothing less. And clothes could range from brands like Esprit, East India Company and Benetton to really upmarket brands like Donna Karan, Valentino, Giorgio Armani and Moschino.

The humble T-shirt is no longer that humble anymore because even T-shirts have got branded labels nowadays, such as the Rock Shop or Hard Rock Cafe. Jeans is another status symbol amongst teens and brands such as Levi's, Guess and Calvin Klein are amongst the favourites.

This brand consciousness, particularly amongst Malaysian teenagers in the urban areas, is a fairly recent phenomenon, originating in the affluent 80s, and gathering momentum in the economically booming 90s. When I was a teenager back in the 70s, there was hardly any of this brand-consciousness at all. Perhaps, brands had not arrived in a big way then nor was there a burgeoning wealthy middle and upper middle class as compared to now. Of course, there were children of wealthy parents in school and some of these teenagers probably wore some things that were a little more expensive than others, but brand names were never ever flaunted. Nor did it ever occur to us then that such things were of any consequence.

I remember we used rubber bands and ribbons to tie our hair into ponytails if it got too long or unruly. Purses and wallets were simple affairs and many of my schoolmates merely carried simple coin pouches. Shoes were mainly from Bata or Fung Keong. These were simple in pattern and had to be washed and whitewashed once a week. In homes where there were schoolgoing children, a familiar sight every weekend would be a row of these shoes, sparkling white and sunning in the sun. Most girls carried their schoolbooks in wicker baskets, whilst boys used canvas knapsacks.

In those days, clothes were relatively cheap. Whoever heard of Giorgio Armani, Donna Karan, Gucci, Sonia Rykiel, Kenzo, Kookai, Naf Naf, Charles Jourdan, Ralph Lauren or Escada then? We were in the aftermath of the turbulent 60s—the restless, soul-searching generation of the Hippie Movement, flower power, the Vietnam War, the Beatles—and were still in its final, twitching throes. Many a teenager cut holes in their jeans and patched them up again with leather or denim, and shredded their T-shirts to resemble tassels—the more hippie-looking and 'groovy' the better. If one looked too neat and proper, one was labelled a 'square'.

Like the adolescent of yesteryear, the adolescent of today is also the same vulnerable, searching child-man or child-woman, sensitive and strongly influenced by peer-group pressure. With all the brand-consciousness and brand talk around him or her, it's hard, I guess, for a teenager not to succumb to the pressure of conforming.

It's fine to enjoy beautiful things in life provided one can afford it, but it becomes ugly and distasteful when it becomes an obsession. There are young teenagers who refuse to wear anything unless it's a designer label, who scowl and fume and rage when Dad or Mum refuses to buy them an expensive brand the name of which they can't even pronounce properly, who demand expensive things in return for scoring good grades in exams.

I know of a teenager who curtly told her mother not to come and fetch her from school because her mother drives a Proton Saga whereas her friends were fetched in BMWs and Mercedes-Benzes. Another teenager brings along a mobile handphone to school, a present from Daddy, so that her boyfriend can call her up for a chat. Too many parents with demanding, high-profile jobs suffer from guilt pangs of not spending enough time with their children and so shower them with money, gifts, supplementary credit cards, and unlimited spending at exclusive clubs.

In the final analysis, the most valuable gift that a parent can give to one's child is a feeling of self-worth and self-esteem that is not dependent on the things that one wears or the brands that one owns but is based on one's values, personal integrity, and abilities, as well as an appreciation of Life, that does not have to be founded on material acquisitions.

48. NURSERY RHYMES
How safe are they?

IT never occurred to me how terribly violent a great deal of nursery rhymes were until I had a child of my own. Often, I would sing or recite to my son these much loved rhymes which I and a great many of my generation had been brought up on. Having to chant these rhymes over and over again, I could not help mulling over their content and that was when I was struck by the fact that there is actually a very high level of violence, cruelty and disaster contained in the rhymes.

Consider the famous lullaby—'Rock a Bye Baby'. First, the baby is placed in a very precarious position—"on the treetop"! When the wind blows, the cradle will rock and "When the bough breaks, the cradle will fall, Down will come baby, cradle and all". Not a particularly comfortable piece of news for Baby considering that one is trying to put the poor fella to sleep.

Remember the other favourite—'Jack and Jill'? How we loved the part where Jack fell down and broke his crown, and Jill came tumbling after! If Jack had actually broken his crown, he would be quite dead as his crown would, I presume, refer to that delicate part around the top of his head. As if this is not horrific enough, what about Humpty Dumpty, that adorable wall-sitter who's always illustrated as an egghead literally. The poor fellow was never quite put together again after falling off the wall.

Protagonists in children's rhymes seem to be beset by a whole load of problems. Consider Little Miss Muffet, the arachnophobic kid who goes into convulsions whenever that dear friendly Spider comes along, or that child pervert, Georgie Porgie, who likes to kiss the girls and make them cry. Yet, when the boys come out to play, the weirdo runs away. As for that kid, little Tommy Tin, he sure sounds as if he has the making of a future serial killer. Remember him, yes, the kid who likes to drown pussycats? And Wee Willie Winkle also has a problem ... running through the streets in his nightgown!

There's also rampant child abuse in the likes of the old woman, the one who lived in the shoe and had so many children, she didn't know what to do, so she gave them some broth without any bread and "whipped them all soundly and sent them to bed". There are gory details such as the blackbird who snapped off the maid's nose in 'Sing a Song of Sixpence' or 'Goosey Goosey Gander' who decided to throw the old man down the stairs because he would not say his prayers! And Arrrggghhhh ... do you remember the farmer's wife who cut off the tails of the 'Three Blind Mice' with a carving knife? How gross!

Still, does it really matter? Are nursery rhymes too about to be condemned just like coffee, sugar, salt, sunbathing and dyed tofu, all considered dangerous for one's health? The truth of the matter is that it really does not matter one bit. Children love nonsense and the more nonsensical, the more enjoyable they seem to find it. A child's mind is a wondrous thing. Only a child can squirm and wriggle with delight when you read to him about the little pig who goes marketing or the cow jumping over the moon. Whoever would have thought that a bunch of Teenage Ninja Turtles, dressed in their underwear, and mutants at that, could have made their creators multi-millionaires overnight?

What's more important is that children simply love rhythm and rhyme. The innate sense of rhythm is a universal thing and children instinctively respond to the sound patterns and cadences of nursery rhymes. Joan Beck (1986), in her book, *How to Raise a Brighter Child*, states that, "Because two- and three-year-olds are so sensitive to language, most of them are fascinated by poetry. Even traditional nursery rhymes—most of which are actually old English political satires which have no meaning for today's children—interest them because of their sound patterns." No wonder then that my two-year-old is able to remember the last words of every other line of the nursery rhyme, "One,

Two, Buckle my ...? "SHOO", he would utter gleefully, not knowing what it all means but relishing the rhythmic flow of the sounds.

So carry on reading those absurdly delightful nursery rhymes and enrich your child's world. I feel Malaysian parents should try, if possible, to impart their knowledge of the rhymes, childhood chants and songs of our Malaysian heritage to our children. Just as we would expect an Irish child to know some Irish rhymes or a Japanese child some Japanese rhymes, shouldn't our children too be familiar with some of what their parents and their parents' parents grew up on? As we rush headlong towards further progress and development, much of our past and what makes us what we are are also inadvertently left behind.

I remember a beautiful childhood rhyme that my mother and my amah used to chant to me, especially on nights when the moon was full. It was a Cantonese chant and it went something like this: *"Yuet kong kong, Chiew tey tong, Lin sam man, Chak pun leong..."* (The moon is bright, Shining down on earth, On New Year's Eve, We'll pluck the beetlenut ...). It went on and on in the most wonderful way and we loved it. I remember too *"Burung Kakak Tua"* which Grandma used to sing to us. We enjoyed the part of the *"gigi-nya tinggal dua"* the most. And Grandpa used to recite to us *pantuns* from his *dondang sayang* days.

So much of our cultural heritage is transmitted verbally and so little of it is recorded that with the passing of time, we tend to forget what we had internalised when we were children. Perhaps we owe it to our future generations to remember and to pass on our own ethnic chants, rhymes, songs and folklore. We should, by all means, enrich our children's lives with all the other worlds that we have in our command, but we should never lose track of what we are and always be proud of what we are.

49. WORKED UP
OVER A CHICKEN

WHEN my child reached his second birthday, I decided to do something that I'd never done before. I resolved to show him what a chicken looked like. No, not those neatly-packed ones covered in plastic cling-wrap and labelled as 'boneless legs', 'keels' or 'chicken necks' at the supermarket, nor those plucked and absolutely dead ones at the wet market, but a real, live chicken.

After all, children's books are full of farm animals, and my little boy had read so many stories of chickens and ducks and cows and goats. And yet, having grown up in the suburbs of Kuala Lumpur, he'd never seen a live chicken before, nor any other poultry animal for that matter.

Surely, I thought, it was time for him to see how a living, breathing, feathered fowl looked like. And I wasn't going to cheat by taking him to the Bird Park or the Zoo either. No, it had to be a real chicken in its true and natural surroundings.

After all, you must have heard the famous (or infamous) story of the kid from Singapore on his first trip to Malaysia. Born and bred in a sophisticated section of the city-state, he'd never been across the causeway before. His parents decided to take him on a trip to Kuantan one day. While driving leisurely along the East Coast road to Kuantan, the child suddenly spotted a cow grazing by the road.

"Oh, look, look!" he yelled excitedly.

"Well what is it, son!" purred his mama proudly, quite sure her well-read son would be able to recognise and identify the animal.

"Oh wow! What a big dog!" the child said.

I resolved that my kid would certainly not become so 'citycised' that he couldn't even tell the difference between a dog and a cow. This Mama would make sure that the child touches base with the 'country' once in a while.

Thus, one morning, we piled a whole load of paraphernalia (try travelling with a two-year-old and you'll know what I mean) into the boot of the car and headed for the nearest beach resort—Port Dickson.

Throughout the journey, there were no chickens to be seen. It was quite understandable along the highways but even after taking the turn-off from the highway, not a single fowl nor four-footed beast was sighted. It was getting easier to sight golf courses than to sight a chicken, I grumbled.

We finally reached our destination—a five-star hotel by the beach. There, ensconced in the lap of luxury, what with room service, Vision 4, piped-in music, the cool inviting pool, waiters pandering to your every beck and call, the clink of elegant china ... I'd quite forgotten all about my original mission statement.

The following day, I remembered my intention. So, we walked to a section of the beach where I remembered there used to be an old bungalow and poultry being reared.

But when we reached the place, I found that everything had been razed and in its place, the beginning of yet another condominium project. On the third and final day of our stay, weary of hotel fare, we ventured out to a coffee-shop at the seventh mile for breakfast.

After a simple breakfast of *nasi lemak*, we were walking towards the car when lo and behold, my son finally saw the first live chicken he'd ever seen in his life. The look of wonder on his face was certainly worth all the chicken-hunting in the world. A skinny, gangly chicken it was, pecking nervously at the soil, not exactly a fine specimen but a scrawny chick was better than none.

My little boy was absolutely thrilled and tailed the chicken. The chicken got the jitters and dashed hysterically into the *kampung* just behind the row of shops, followed by the toddler and his parents. The *pak cik* sitting on the verandah of a house nearby smiled in a benign way, probably wondering why these city slickers seemed to be getting more and more *ulu* (uncivilised) by the day, getting all worked up over a skinny-looking hen.

Later that day, we returned home, feeling quite satisfied. Our mission had been accomplished and we were back in the urban jungle of Kuala Lumpur. I'm thinking of getting out to the country again this weekend—now to look for a cow ...

50. THE JADED CHILD

A weekend ago, I brought my fourteen-year-old niece and some friends on a picnic in the countryside. A lovely picnic spot it was, beside a stream that cascaded into a pool, and bordered by picturesque boulders. All around us was the unruffled green forest, its tall trees and abundant ferns a solace to stressed-out city souls. I was in seventh heaven.

I looked around for my niece. She was perched on a boulder in the stream. After five minutes, with an utterly droll expression, she looked up at me and said, "What do we do next? I'm bored."

"Bored? Did I hear you say you're bored? How can all these beauty around you be boring?" asked the flabbergasted aunt.

"But there's nothing to do out here."

"But that's precisely it. Nothing to do but to enjoy Nature. Isn't it beautiful here? Look, just look at those dragonflies hovering over the water. Look at the colours of their wings, and look at the butterflies sipping water at the rock pool right next to you."

"So boring, I should have brought my mini compo and my New Kids on the Block tape."

I gulped in disbelief. Somehow, having NKOTB blasting away in my tranquil retreat wasn't exactly my idea of a day of communion with Mother Nature.

Children have it so good nowadays, haven't they? At the tender age of Nothing, whilst still in the womb, they are already entertained to the strains of Mozart and Chopin, and if you have the stomach for it, NKOTB. There are also commercially-produced womb music tapes which child psychologists say help to stimulate the child's development.

Then, when the baby is born, the stimulation from the womb world to the real world increases. There are the most imaginative musical mobiles that tinkle out lullabies while twirling round and round. To stimulate the child further, there are toys for the cot, for the baby walker, and for the baby chair. And the range of books for babies is incredible: cloth books, wipe-away books, books for the bathtub, books that sing, books that pop up, sticker books.

Never mind if the babies can't understand a word of what you're blabbering about, just keep on reading to them—you'll be rewarded one day, you'll see.

The toys that children get nowadays make those that the children of the 1950s and early 1960s had quite laughable. The toys we had then were things like a wad of cards, a marble or two, rubber bands, a simple plastic *masak-masak* set, a kite, a top, a skipping rope, which kept us happily occupied for hours. Many toys even came free such as fighting spiders, five stones, a hopscotch pattern scrawled on the sand.

Today, all you've got to do to get an idea of the state-of-the-art situation in Toyland is to step into Toys 'R' Us. For the adult first-timer, it can be quite a culture shock. No friendly little toy shop here. Instead you find yourself in a cavernous store, filled to the brim with thousands of toys.

After wandering about for hours in the jungle of toys, you emerge green with envy at all the toys you never had, and feeling every inch the deprived adult! (No wonder you see these 'unaccompanied' adults sometimes, hovering between the shelves, surreptitiously playing away with the toys when they think no one is looking!)

In Toys 'R' Us, you'll notice that it is the adults, and not the children, who walk about with a look of amazement in their eyes. You'll also notice that the mothers of today buy toys as if they're doing their weekly grocery shopping, piling toys into the pushcart trolleys and wheeling them to the checkout counter without blinking an eye.

As the children grow older, why, it's time to go to school! When I say "grow older", I don't mean old as in 'six years old' ... now, that's really old! I mean 'old' as in *two* years old or *three* years old. When you're that old, it's time to go to playschool or nursery school. Sitting around

206

in the house till you're six would be courting disaster. A yuppified six-year-old kid today can count from 1 to 100 in two or three languages, sing A to Z in one breath, add and subtract in the blink of an eye, play a musical instrument and handle the computer mouse as deftly as a cat can handle the real thing.

At playschool, the children learn to innovate, create, socialise and relate. They learn sensorial skills, motor co-ordination skills, word recognition skills, reading and mathematical skills. It's all these child development literature in the market that is causing this toddler-education phenomenon.

Child experts warn of the dire consequences if you miss out on those most crucial years of a child's life, between two and five years of age. They say that during this period, a child's mind absorbs everything like a sponge. After that, no matter what you do, his fate is sealed. Besides, what if it's true? What if your child's mind is truly like a thirsty sponge, thirsting for stimulation? You don't want to be accused of intellectual malnourishment of your own child, do you?

Some parents take the task of stimulating and educating their children quite seriously. They spend thousands of ringgit on reading packages, educational video tapes, children's encyclopaedias, computer software and tuition classes. They send their children to camps, workshops and special courses.

One little eight-year-old girl I know seldom comes out to play because she is so busy trying to keep up with her homework and tuition classes. Tuition has become a big business. Tuition first started out in this country as special coaching for students weak in a particular subject, for example, Malay or Additional Mathematics. But now, many children are sent to tuition classes for just about every subject under the sun. There's even tuition to cope with tuition! On top of that, there are all the other things that parents never had as children and want to give their children such as music, ballet, swimming and art lessons. Then there are the vital skills that children facing the 21st century need such as computer classes and if there's any time left, Mandarin classes ("China's the next economic giant, you know," they tell you).

When I recall the things that the children of my childhood did from ages two to five, it's a wonder that we aren't all duds today. We never had all this stimulation that the children today are receiving. All we had were trees to climb, sand to play with, drains and streams where we caught guppies and tadpoles, and strange though as it may sound to children nowadays, we got quite stimulated whacking away at a pile of cardboard cards for hours with an old slipper.

Yes, children today are really lucky. Parents are better informed and more affluent and will leave no stone unturned to ensure that their children get the best that life has to offer. But in our zeal, we have got to be careful. We must strike a balance and allow our children to grow at their own natural pace. They have got to have some space of their own and some time to be what they are. There is nothing more jaded in this world than a jaded child.

51. SEX EDUCATION
IN THE 1970s

I read in the papers the other day that, finally, with the spectre of AIDS looming in the background, the decision has been made to teach sex education in our schools. Our young people have to know the facts of life. It isn't so much a question of innocence unnecessarily lost at such a tender age; it's a question of life and death nowadays. Knowing the facts may help save lives.

Back in school in the 1970s, there wasn't such immense pressure to educate teenagers about the facts of life. In fact, there was nothing remotely near sex education at all. One just picked up delicious morsels of information from whispered conversations along school corridors, or from romance novels by Denise Robbins and Barbara Cartland. That didn't help very much either as the heroines in romance novels those days remained virtuous till the very end. On the brink of losing her chastity to the lecherous villain, the heroine was always rescued by the dashing hero, naturally.

The only thing that was remotely similar to a sex education lesson was a page in the General Science textbook for the third form, entitled "Fertilisation". This complex topic was covered in three scanty paragraphs on just half a single page, followed by a picture of a rabbit with its insides exposed. From this, we were expected to deduce all the secrets and mysteries of procreation, as well as learn about the male and female bodies—all by peering into the private parts of a rabbit! I remember it was on the last page of the Biology section of the book, which was followed by the Chemistry and Physics sections.

For one whole term, we studied Biology—focusing specifically on the outer and inner parts of plants and flowers. Everything we ever wanted to learn about the balsam plant but were afraid to ask, we received in full measure. We collected balsam, planted balsam, dissected balsam, drew balsam, memorised balsam parts till we became green in the face with balsam! Then, it was the hibiscus—we learnt about its sepals, epi sepals, stalk, stem, filament and pollen grains. We had hibiscus day in, day out till it was sprouting out of our ears!

Eagerly, we waited for that day when our Science teacher would teach us all about fertilisation. By now, we had become walking experts on how plants fertilised themselves—through wind, water and air. Still, we couldn't make the connection from the flora world to the fauna world. Why on earth was the teacher taking such a long time tiptoeing through the tulips when we were dying to learn the sordid facts about fertilisation, and not pollination?

Finally, one morning, our time had arrived. The last paragraph on the plant kingdom had been explained to death the day before. We knew that on this day, our Science teacher had to—she just had to—move on to the next topic—fertilisation! We could hear her footsteps down the corridor. "She's coming! She's coming!" yelled our lookout, and we dashed back to our seats, all forty-five of us girls trying to look like innocent angelic darlings thirsting for knowledge, regardless of whatever kind.

In walked the Science mistress, Miss Chou, an excellent teacher who never failed us. She was single, in her forties, and of a prim and proper disposition. She was the type who pronounced all her Ps and Ts clearly and was always dressed in cotton blouses with prudish Peter Pan collars. She looked at the forty-five faces all transfixed on her, eyes wide open, agog with attention, forty-five blossoming young ladies, hanging on to her every word, their books neatly turned to the page where the rabbits lay. We couldn't believe our ears when Miss Chou gave us a disgusted look and said, "I know you girls are dying to learn about fertilisation. Well, there are plenty of books on the subject in the library, so go and read it up yourselves. I am not going to touch on this topic. If you are so interested, go read all about it ... Let's move on to the next subject—Chemistry.

"The chemical name for water is H$_2$O, which is two parts hydrogen and one part oxygen ..."

Blah, blah, blah ...

And so, from greenery, we launched right into gases, our faces crestfallen, our spirits crushed, but our innocence preserved yet a little longer.

Today, life has become so much more complex and AIDS a real threat. Don't beat around the balsams too long. Teach and equip our teenagers with the facts so that they may choose life and live to smell the flowers.

LIFESTYLES

52. FOR THE LOVE OF SINGING

WHEN the Japanese occupied Malaya three score and ten years ago, they made it mandatory for all Malayans to learn the language of the conquerors. Everyone had to learn Japanese known as Nippongo at that time. Thus, today, there are a number of Malaysians in their 50s and above who can remember vaguely a smattering of Japanese. I myself learnt a Japanese word from my parents and that is, the word, *bakelo*, which means 'bloody fool'! My parents told me they remember this word distinctly because the Japanese soldiers, during the Japanese Occupation, often used this word on the civilians, when bullying or scolding them, or about to chop off their heads.

Today, Malaysians have become quite familiar with a fairly new Japanese word *karaoke* which means 'with own orchestra'. Surprisingly, Malaysians who are by nature quite shy and inhibited in public, have taken to this pastime in a big way. If in the past, the Japanese conquered our land but never our hearts and minds, well, today, *karaoke* has certainly conquered our hearts. You could even call it a worldwide invasion for it has become very popular in many countries of the world. From the land of the Eskimoes to the Land Down Under, *karaoke* has become quite an in-thing. Thanks to Japanese ingenuity, *karaoke* has made many a secret fantasy come true. From out of the woodwork, great singers, mediocre ones, half-baked ones and absolutely deplorable and 'goosepimple-inducing' ones have come to the fore, clasped the microphone and with a full orchestral backing from the *karaoke* set, savoured those few sweet moments of magic when the rest of the world had to stop to listen.

It is really quite interesting to observe the behaviour of people who have decided to have a *karaoke* get-together at a *karaoke* lounge. Initially, the mike keeps getting passed around as everyone feels a little shy and reserved. The 'green horns' especially will make all sorts of excuses like "No-*lah*, this song doesn't fit my voice," or "Cannot-*lah*. My voice doesn't fit this song," or "I got a sore throat," or "The pitch is too high for me-*lah*" or "The beat is too slow-*lah*". Or one could also start blaming the tools, for example, "This mike is so lousy-*lah!*" or "So many spelling mistakes on the screen ... How to sing?"! But there is something magical about *karaoke* because by the end of the session, everyone is practically fighting for the microphone and for his turn to sing!

The choice of songs is tremendous at the more expensive and classier *karaoke* joints. There are sheets of titles of songs listed in alphabetical order, filed in clearholders which you have to flick through. Just choose the song you like and punch in the number of the song into a boxlike receiver and eventually your song will appear on the TV screen. Songs are not just in English but there is also a choice of Malay, Chinese, Indian and Japanese songs.

There are basically four types of *karaoke* singers: those who can sing and know it, those who can sing but don't know it, those who can't sing and know it, and finally those who can't sing but don't know it. Listening to those from the first category is a pleasure, of course. The singer is supremely confident and knows his audience is spellbound thus spurring him on to greater heights. Listening to a singer from the second category is often a pleasant surprise with the singer the most pleasantly surprised of all!

As for the third category, because he knows he can't sing, he is usually quite considerate and tries not to hog the microphone too much, going for the easier numbers such as Stevie Wonder's *I Just Called To Say I Love You* or popular evergreens like *Five Hundred Miles* although sometimes he might get tempted to do Frank Sinatra's *My Way* on his captive audience. Basically, he tries not to be too much of a pain.

It is those from the last category (yes, those who can't sing but don't know it) that are the most painful to endure. Howling, screeching, droning, singing off-key, inflecting wrongly, yowling, groaning and cackling—all the hi-fi technology that the Japanese have mustered and poured so lovingly into creating this thing called the *karaoke* set, alas, still cannot help this category of people.

But, if the fact that a bad singer is ... period ... a bad singer, even with the help of a *karaoke*, the good thing is that it teaches tolerance. No matter how bad you are, no one ever boos, swears or throws rotten eggs at you. Your audience will sit through and listen either in bemused or morbid fascination. And at the end of your delivery (and their deliverance), you might even be loudly applauded just for having made the attempt.

A friend posed an interesting question to me the other day at a wedding dinner. A guest was singing his lungs out Julie Roger's *The Wedding* via *karaoke*. "What do you think? Was *karaoke* invented for people who can sing but never had the chance or was it invented to give a chance to those who can't sing?"

Well, I guess it's meant for all, whether nightingales or larks or just plain *gagaks* (crows). It's not the degree of talent that matters in *karaoke*, it's the degree of guts.

53. RAZZMATAZZ AT MALAYSIAN WEDDINGS

T HE famous Wedding March 'Here Comes the Bride' is being played. The radiant bride and happy groom glide, march or stumble into the restaurant or the ballroom, depending on how they interpret the Wedding March, and take their seats to the applause of guests. The guests also take their seats, heaving sighs of relief, and wait expectantly for the food to arrive. After all, it has been a long wait. No matter the inclusion of the word 'sharp' for the arrival time on the wedding invitation card, Malaysians seem quite blunt to it and still persistently arrive late for such functions.

Suddenly, all the lights go off and no, no, it's not a power failure. It's that gimmick again ... you know, the gimmick that started off as a gimmick by the hotels but has never died off since and from the looks of it, might just become a tradition.

"Ba Da Da Ta Da aah ... Ba Da Da Ta Da aah" ... vigorous drum rolls ... followed by more "BaDaDahs" which incidentally is the introduction of the 'BaDaDah' song by the Ray Coniff Singers. Even more popular are the theme songs from Hollywood movies such as *Raiders of the Lost Ark*, *Star Wars*, or *Superman*.

Whatever the choice may be, the music is usually played extremely loudly. If you're in a grand ballroom, just like the Academy Awards Presentations, the searchlights go flickering over the heads of the guests gathered there. The music rises to a crescendo and oooohhh, What is it? what is it? what? what? In case you're dying of suspense, it's just that, ladies and gentlemen, dinner is served.

In the darkness, the waiters and waitresses, in a procession, march in, each carrying the first course of the meal, lit with a candle. They march up to the front of the hall, turn around, face the guests and with the music still rumbling away, they bow and then the lights come on and they serve the food.

There are many variations to this. Sometimes you may have the waiters coming in with flaming torches in their hands. Sometimes, the waiters come in each holding an ice sculpture, lit up with a little torch light. The competition must be heating up because at the last two wedding dinners I attended, these 'servings' seemed to be getting even more far-fetched than ever.

At the first one, the lights went out followed by a terrible roar of a plane. It got louder and louder and sounded as if it were just overhead and then a waiter, complete with a parachute arrived and served the first dish to the bridal couple! At the second one, to the theme song of *The Last Emperor*, a 'coolie' huffed and puffed and pulled in a red rickshaw. A pretty maiden stepped out with a dish of Four Seasons in her arms, walked up to the main table, served the dish, then left in the rickshaw, Four Seasons lighter!

The idea behind these 'presentations' is basically a good one. In a banquet or feast, food should be served with great aplomb and ceremony. But as with all things to do with pomp and aplomb, they are only stunningly effective provided they are executed dramatically and with great precision and timing. Otherwise they can look rather corny, and one wonders why they have not died a natural death.

At a dinner I attended, some of the guests nearly died of a heart attack—the flaming torch that the waiter was carrying got quite out of control and the waiter looked as if he was going to ditch the burning javelin-like thing at the guests. And at another, flanked by two waiters holding burning torches, the head waiter had to wheel in a heavy trolley bearing the first course, covered with a silver lid. The trolley behaved badly, squeaking and groaning, and its wheels kept going sideways resulting in the poor waiter moving like a crab down the aisle.

At yet another, after the lights went out, a voice came over the air in a tone as if announcing the gladiatorial games of Rome, "Let the Dinner begin". We waited and waited, and yet dinner did not materialise. The voice came on again, "Ahem ... Let the Dinner begin ... I said ... let the Dinner begin ..." That must have been the cue for the waiters to march in. Perhaps they were still not in their positions or maybe the kitchen was too far from the ballroom. Perhaps, the cooks were in a bad mood that night and deliberately delayed dinner and so we had to wait in the darkness for a while before dinner finally began ... but not before flaming torches, more ice sculptures, flickering candlelights and what was it? ... yes, I think it was the theme from *Mission Impossible* this time.

54. BELIEVING IN NUMBERS

W HEN buying a new car, Malaysian Chinese are more particular about the registration number compared to other Malaysians. For example, a Malay or an Indian would think nothing of driving a car with the plate 4444, but the Chinese would prefer not to own this number. Numbers have always been regarded by the Chinese as significant as they are believed to be linked with the cosmological system. According to Evelyn Lip, a *feng shui* expert in her book, *Chinese Numbers*, numbers represent the *xing* (the nine *xing* which symbolise the essence of the universe) and the Five Elements (gold, wood, water, fire and earth under which all things on earth are classified).

Numbers also represent the eight directional orientations, as well as possess masculine and feminine qualities. All odd numbers are considered masculine (*yang*) and all even numbers feminine (*ying*). Therefore, to the Chinese mind, numbers are not just figures; they also carry special meaning and symbolism.

The Chinese are particular about the sounds of numbers as the sounds may suggest good or bad luck. Thus, the number 4 is disliked as it sounds very much like *sei*, which means 'die' in the Cantonese dialect. Numbers such as 14 or 1414 would certainly not augur well for the potential car owner as the number 1 sounds like 'sure' and 4 sounds like 'to die'. This would mean that one is driving around with a number that implies that one is 'sure to die'! Or in the case of 1414, doubly sure to die! Other similar permutations such as 1114 and 4441 would mean more or less the same imminent death message.

A combination of the number 2 and the number 4 is frowned upon, as 2 is pronounced as *yi* in Cantonese which means 'easy'. Therefore, a number such as 2424 would mean 'easy to die' which to a superstitious person would surely be quite stressful. Imagine his anxiety if he gets a number such as 1124! Other unfavourable combinations are the number 2324 which implies 'easy to live, easy to die'; and the number 5354 which sounds like 'neither dead nor alive' in Cantonese.

Therefore, rather than get an unlucky number, many Chinese, particularly members of the business community, are willing to pay good money to tender for a 'good' number.

The most well-liked numbers by the Chinese are the numbers 8 and 9. 8 is regarded as a lucky number by the Chinese, as it sounds like *fa* (to multiply). Car registration numbers like 8888 or 1818 are in great demand as they symbolise great prosperity. A number like 128 is a popular number as it indicates 'easy to succeed'. Moreover, it is a *yang-yin-yang* number and so it is considered smooth and auspicious. The number 4 is only acceptable if it is combined with 8, resulting in the number 48 which means that one will 'prosper to the end'.

The number 9 (*jiu*) is a very auspicious number. It symbolises the Metal Element and the West direction. It is the last of the *yang* numbers and represents longevity. A registration number such as 9999 is highly valued, and businessmen are willing to pay hundreds of dollars to bid for this number.

This belief in the symbolism of numbers is also prevalent when buying houses. Addresses with numbers such as 8 or 18 or 128 would certainly be favoured. Although the number 13 in Cantonese implies 'sure to grow' or 'liveliness', Western superstitions have exerted some influence and Malaysian Chinese who observe numerology are wary of this number, and believe it to be an unlucky number. Have you noticed that in some hotels and office blocks, there are no floors numbered 13, and in some housing estates, there are no houses numbered 13? (They are numbered 11b or 12b instead.)

Well, no wonder then that the share market is rather quiet these days for as one superstitious friend, who got 'burned' at the beginning of this year, told me, "I should have known better than to play the market; it's 1994! 1-9-9-4 in Cantonese sounds like 'once you play, sure to die!'" If one operates by that line of thinking, just imagine how bullish the market will get in four years' time when it's 1998!

55. THE LURE OF
THE KOPI TIAM

THE local coffeeshop or *kopi tiam* in Hokkien is a ubiquitous feature of Malaysian life. Most of us have a favourite coffeeshop near our home or workplace where we like to pop in for a cup of *kopi-O* or a bite. Somewhat like the pub in the TV sitcom *Cheers*, where if you frequent it often enough, it becomes a place where everybody knows your face, though not necessarily your name.

Names aren't particularly important in the *kopi tiam* culture; nobody asks for your name, and neither will you quite know the names of the hawkers in the coffeeshop because they are usually called by the name of the food they sell. For example, you call so-and-so Char Kway Teow because he sells *char kway teow*, or you call the lady manning the stall at the front of the shop Chee Cheong Fun because she sells the stuff, and you call the *satay* man Satay. It might sound terribly rude to a foreigner, calling people by the names of food, but it's all quite acceptable in the world of the *kopi tiam*.

The *kopi tiam* is devoid of any fanciful decor, and that by itself gives it its own special atmosphere. There are no stylish chairs or tables, no uniforms and no air-conditioning; everything is strictly utilitarian. In the old days, you would find marble tables, with spitoons underneath. The marble tables are now considered 'hot' antiques and have mostly been sold away to ardent collectors who won't hesitate to coax the owner to a sale on the spot. These days, tabletops are usually formica. Beer ads, featuring attractive Oriental beauties in low-cut gowns and high slits, are usually plastered on the walls, boxes are stacked at odd corners, and at the back of the shop, there's always a gigantic silver-coloured fridge.

The number of stalls in a coffeeshop can range anywhere from two or three to twenty, depending on its size. The food sold is usually Chinese hawker fare, but can be quite multicultural, such as *nasi lemak*, *roti canai*, hot dog, *ikan panggang*, steak, chicken chop, fish and chips, etc. The choices available in a coffeeshop are incredible—Hainanese chicken rice, Penang prawn mee, fishball soup, Penang *loh bak*, *kon low mee*, *assam laksa*, *chee cheong fun*, *bak kut teh*, Teow Chew porridge ... the list is virtually endless.

What I find most remarkable about the *kopi tiam* are the people working there. They toil seven days a week. They are up by 5.00 A.M. and on their feet till about 3.00 P.M. Some stop for a rest in the afternoon and then start again for the night session. Unlike salaried workers, they have no EPF, medical coverage, house loans, car loans or annual leave to shout about. They usually take one break a year, during the festive season. They don't have fancy menus, nor do they take orders with the aid of notebooks and pens. They just look at the customer when he places an order, and somehow the dish he orders will reach him in a matter of minutes.

I don't know how the system works but I think the hawker takes a photographic imprint of the customer in his mind. When the time comes to deliver the food, one can hear the hawker tell his assistant, usually a family member, to bring it to 'the lady with two kids', or the *sei ngan chai* (Cantonese for the 'four-eyed fella'), or the *lang nui* (Cantonese for 'pretty girl') or *Si-Botak tu* (Malay for the 'bald one there').

What always astounds me is how the hawker can remember all the various permutations without once having to write them down. For example, he may be given an order of *char kway teow* without any chilli, but with more *taugeh* (bean sprouts). The next moment, another order is placed—this time "with lots of chilli, please, a bit of *taugeh* but leave out the cockles"! Another person comes along and places four more orders with different combinations. Try standing in front of the noodle stalls and you'll find the permutations even more confusing, what with the different types of noodle available—fat mee, thin mee, flat mee, *meehoon*, *kway teow*, *loh see fun*, and the different accompaniments—with or without chicken, pork, mushroom, fish-ball, liver, chilli, vegetables, etc.

Have you ever seen the hawker pausing to write the orders down? I certainly haven't! Somehow, he stores them all in his head. He cannot afford to make a mistake as it could be costly—he just might end up getting a scolding or have the dish returned. Talk about memory skills and mind control; these hawkers have certainly mastered the technique without having attended a single seminar in their lives!

In the *kopi tiam*, the setting is friendly, casual and noisy. Customers stroll in dressed in whatever garb they fancy and can stay for however long they like. A lot of noise is generated by the guy taking the orders for drinks as his method of relaying the information is simple—just holler at the top of his voice, "*Kopi-O noh* ..." (two black coffee) or "Milo!", and the person manning the drinks counter will instantly pick up the cue.

Malaysians are real lucky; we still get to eat our food served in porcelain or plastic bowls with real spoons, chopsticks and cutlery, and drinks come in real glasses or porcelain cups and saucers. In Singapore, most hawker fare come in styrofoam bowls. I feel miserable every time I've to eat out of styrofoam. More hygienic perhaps, but give me food in authentic bowls any time.

I have my own favourite *kopi tiam*. The food there is superb, mainly authentic Penang hawker fare. The hawkers there speak Hokkien and are friendly in a non-intrusive way. Sitting there sipping my coffee, I feel at home for I'm surrounded by familiar faces. Like the pubs, country clubs, hotel lounges and restaurants, the humble coffeeshop also plays an important role—a place for sustenance, relaxation and interaction. Long may it live!

56. GETTING AN EARFUL

HERE'S a list of people whom I've seen with a mobile telephone: the butcher, the baker, the candlestick maker, the fishmonger, the chicken seller, the *pasar malam* hawker, the mechanic, the electrician, the plumber, the contractor, the insurance agent, the remisier, the businessman, the manager, the CEO, the housewife, the student and the socialite.

Almost everybody from all walks of life in the cities seems to own a mobile telephone nowadays. The only group of people whom I've seldom seen with handphones are the senior citizens. Perhaps this category of people have managed all their lives without handphones and can't see why at this time of their lives they should do with them.

When Alexander Graham Bell invented the telephone, I'm sure he didn't foresee the day when the telephone would become so terribly indispensable. From those gentle slow-paced days when the telephone was something you placed discreetly in the corner of your living room, to pick up once in a while when it let out a tinkle, it has now grown to such importance that it is practically hinged around some people's ears and mouths.

Just take a drive along the average highway in Kuala Lumpur at peak traffic conditions and you'll see countless motorists with this contraption called the handphone glued to their ears and mouths. Sit in a restaurant or coffeeshop and chances are you'll hear one person jabbering away into his handphone.

Attend a meeting or a conference and you'll hear the shrill trilling of someone's handphone. Quite a number of schoolchildren carry handphones to school, I was told, so that their parents can keep track of their whereabouts. A schoolgirl I know carries a handphone to school and when the lesson gets too boring to bear, phones up her boy-friend to chat!

At a recent workshop which I facilitated, the executive ran out of the room right in the midst of his presentation when his handphone rang, so conditioned had he become in responding to it.

At the *pasar tani*, just the other day, a housewife, right in the midst of choosing *ikan kembong*, called home to find out from the maid how her darling daughter was getting along without Mummy. I stood there, gaping, astounded at the many versatile uses and the power of this newfangled thing called the mobile telephone.

I have nothing against the mobile telephone. It is a symbol of the times we live in. Indeed it is a marvellous invention and a boon for people who have to be constantly on the move. Time, for many, is money and being contactable may make all the difference, especially in a city like Kuala Lumpur where one spends half of one's life caught in traffic jams.

But I sure have something against people who do not practise common telephone etiquette. Ever tried sitting down to a meal in a nice restaurant only to find the customer next to you yelling into his handphone? Or try to enjoy some music at a lounge somewhere only to be subjected to a businessman cutting a deal through his hand-phone a metre away?

Last weekend, at a Chinese restaurant, I felt sorry for the group of people at the table next to mine. The host was on the handphone throughout the meal, making one call after another! How annoying it must have been for the rest of the group for, I noticed, it was quite im-possible for them to converse what with their phone-fixated friend speaking at the top of his voice.

One wonders why he even bothered to gather all his *kakis* for a meal when in the end he preferred the company of his handphone. Or—forgive my cynicism—was it to show off and to impress on how important one or one's business had become, that fellowship with one's friends could be suspended in favour of solving operational prob-lems or cutting the deal?

On another occasion, at the waiting room of a doctor's clinic, all seven sick and bleary-eyed patients, including myself, had to listen to a patient, also waiting like us, admonish his subordinate through his handphone on how to run the office. He sat in the middle of the room, his illness quite forgotten, and ranted into the phone. He did not seem to care a jot about the fact that there were others in the room—and quite sick ones too—and that we might not be in the mood for noise, so engrossed was he in his conversation. Eavesdropping is bad enough but *enforced* eavesdropping! After ten minutes, all seven of us had learnt all about his office politics.

Perhaps the handphone is something so recent that the etiquette on how to use it hasn't quite sunk in yet. Common sense would dictate though that the owner should rule it and not the other way round. Common sense would also indicate that a telephone conversation, whether fixed or mobile, should be a private affair. The whole world need not have to be forced to listen.

57. CHANGING RULES OF DATING RITUAL

Just within four generations, the dating and courtship patterns of the young have changed quite a bit. My niece, in her late teens, doesn't agonise too much—if she's interested in a guy, she'll call him up and chat with him on the phone. If she really likes him, she might even ask him out on a date. During 'my time', back in the mid-1970s, it just wasn't done. No matter how much you liked the guy, you still didn't make the first move. You could hint or flirt, but seldom did a girl do the wooing and chasing.

Dating was unheard of during my grandparents' time. The Nyonyas of three to four generations ago did not have much say on their marriage partners. Most marriages were arranged, and one only got to know one's life partner after one had gotten hitched. My grandmother was married off at the tender age of fourteen, after only three years of formal education, to a man twelve years older. His mother, quite an ogre of a lady, felt that her bachelor son was getting too randy for her liking and decided to marry him off. She found the perfect match for her son in my grandmother, a young Peranakan beauty, just merely a year or two past puberty. By the time she reached twenty years of age, she already had three children. From a mere child, she had to take on immediately the roles of wife, mother and daughter-in-law. Many women in those days never had the luxury of girlhood—that special transitory time when a girl gradually blossoms into a woman, enjoying life and all its joys and pleasures.

Grandma was an intelligent and capable woman. How must it have been like, I wonder, to have so little say in one's life? Whereas women today would ask themselves questions about what they want out of life, did she and her contemporaries never have their own

233

dreams on how their life's course should be? Did they never wonder about self-actualisation, or was it a concept which did not even exist then? Was love all a matter of conditioning and not a matter of the heart? What if love never came after marriage? Or is love dependent really on the circumstances and the choices available? When one has no choice, one just has to love what one has.

My mother was more fortunate. She married the man she loved. My father was smitten by a photograph of her which he chanced upon in a friend's album. The photograph was a picture of a young girl with big eyes and a rather serious expression, standing beside a peacock's pride tree. He fell in love with the girl in the photograph. After a few discreet inquiries, he found out who she was, where she lived and henceforth, set about to woo the girl who had captured his heart. It so happened that their families were mutual friends. My mother liked him too—this tall and shy man who didn't have many words to say. Courtship then was a highly chaperoned affair. Times together were spent reading books, playing badminton with friends and strolling around BB Park—a popular amusement centre where Sungei Wang Plaza is now located—always in the company of aunties and sisters. They never went out together until after they got married.

It wasn't the lack of opportunity that hindered my mother from her dream of further education after her Senior Cambridge. It was the Japanese Occupation of Malaya. The arrival of the Japanese completely dashed her plans. She and her sisters had to flee to the countryside, hide from roving bands of Japanese soldiers looking for *ku niang* (Mandarin for "maiden"), cover themselves with dirt and look as repulsive as possible. She continued her own education during the war years by reading whatever books she could lay her hands on. She did most of her reading by the light of a bicycle lamp. Often, the air raid sirens would sound, and the whole place had to be blacked out. She loved Shakespeare, and I have often been astounded by how she could quote chunks of Shakespeare, whenever she felt like it, particularly from *The Tempest*, her favourite.

Long after the war ended, she refused to buy anything Japanese. Electrical appliances in my home were all either British or American or

European-made, and the cars we owned were a Hillman, followed by a Volvo, and lastly, a Chrysler Avenger. My mother's policy of "Buy Japanese Last" was adhered to until she was in her sixties and there wasn't much of anything else to buy. Her last fridge, an European model, was almost rusting to bits but still, she refused to buy a new one. Her first and last electrical appliance, made with Japanese technology, was a microwave oven. By then, I guess, her bitterness towards the Japanese had somewhat ebbed.

When it came to my turn in the dating game, I was free to go out with whoever I liked, provided of course, the person I liked made the initiative. Girls from my generation just didn't ask guys out. Somehow, it didn't even occur to us to ask, "And why not?" You could send out signals, make eye contact, flutter whatever eyelashes you had until you go batty, but if the guy didn't respond, you just gave up. Period.

Things weren't so strict anymore compared to my mother's time but it wasn't particularly straightforward either. I had to ask permission from my mother, who would then ask permission from my father. Father would get back to me with a set of questions about the gentleman whom his daughter was going out with. I still remember his questions: "What is his name?", "What does he do?, "What school does he come from?" and for some strange reason to me at that time, Father wanted to know "What does his father do?"

When the poor suitor arrived, he would be scrutinised, and then my father would grunt the same questions again. He would try to make it sound as though he was just making polite conversation, but it sure sounded like an interrogation. It helped if the gentleman in question was educated at the Victoria Institution as it was my father's *alma mater*, and he was terribly partial to anything from his old school.

Curfew hours would then be stipulated and I remember whenever I came home, Mother would always be there, waiting, unable to sleep until I came home. If I did not come home at the stipulated time, it wasn't beyond her to start calling up the local hospitals. I used to resent her waiting up for me. I was young and I wanted to feel free and independent without someone watching over me all the time. Being a mother myself now, I can understand the anxiety she must have gone through, when her child, no matter how old, had not come home. I wish I could tell her now how much I understand and appreciate the meaning of motherhood and the cost it carries, but she passed away before I became a mother.

So, if one looks at the patterns through the generations, women have indeed come a long way today. Each generation empowers the next. Education is a right and not a privilege. With education and economic independence, we are free to lead our lives according to our own choices and decisions. Matrimony is a highly personal choice and choosing to remain single is considered quite normal nowadays.

The other day, I overheard my niece Jean asking a boy out on a date. I felt like a dinosaur or 'something' from the past, when I asked her a barrage of questions.

"How's it like asking a guy out on a date? Don't you feel nervous? What if he thinks you're *hadap* (hard up)? You mean the young men today don't mind being pursued by the female?"

The precocious young lady answered, "I don't see why only the males should have the right to make the first move when they like someone. Why can't females have that right too? Besides, terms like 'pursuing' and 'being pursued' are sexist."

I smiled and shrugged. I won't be surprised that one day when she has a daughter, the women of her daughter's generation will be the ones making the marriage proposals first, probably via fax or e-mail!

LEE SU KIM

Malaysian Flavours

INSIGHTS INTO THINGS MALAYSIAN

Pelanduk
Publications

Published by
Pelanduk Publications (M) Sdn. Bhd.,
24 Jalan 20/16A, 46300 Petaling Jaya,
Selangor Darul Ehsan, Malaysia.

Address all correspondence to
Pelanduk Publications (M) Sdn. Bhd.,
P.O. Box 8265, 46785 Kelana Jaya,
Selangor Darul Ehsan, Malaysia.

Ist printing April 1996
2nd printing September 1996

Perpustakaan Negara Malaysia   Cataloguing-in-Publication Data

Lee, Su Kim
    Malaysian flavours: insights into
    things Malaysian / Lee Su Kim.
    ISBN 967-978-517-3
    1. Malaysia—Social life and customs. I. Title.
    306.09595

Printed in Malaysia by
Laser Press Sdn. Bhd.